Rule of t

MW01701508

The Rule of the SACRED HEART

Finding Rest in a Restless World

Leonard J. DeLorenzo

Our Sunday Visitor
Huntington, Indiana

Nihil Obstat
Msgr. Michael Heintz, Ph.D.
Censor Librorum

Imprimatur
✠ Kevin C. Rhoades
Bishop of Fort Wayne-South Bend
January 26, 2026

The *Nihil Obstat* and *Imprimatur* are official declarations that a book is free from doctrinal or moral error. It is not implied that those who have granted the *Nihil Obstat* and *Imprimatur* agree with the contents, opinions, or statements expressed.

Excerpts from the *Revised Standard Version of the Bible*—Second Catholic Edition (Ignatius Edition) Copyright © 2006 National Council of the Churches of Christ in the United States of America. Used by permission. All rights reserved worldwide.

Every reasonable effort has been made to determine copyright holders of excerpted materials and to secure permissions as needed. If any copyrighted materials have been inadvertently used in this work without proper credit being given in one form or another, please notify Our Sunday Visitor in writing so that future printings of this work may be corrected accordingly.

Copyright © 2026 by Leonard J. DeLorenzo

31 30 29 28 27 26   2 3 4 5 6 7 8 9

All rights reserved. With the exception of short excerpts for critical reviews, no part of this work may be reproduced or transmitted in any form or by any means whatsoever without permission from the publisher. For more information, visit: www.osv.com/permissions.

Our Sunday Visitor Publishing Division
Our Sunday Visitor, Inc.
200 Noll Plaza
Huntington, IN 46750
www.osv.com
1-800-348-2440

ISBN: 978-1-63966-412-2   (Inventory No. T3030)
1. RELIGION—Christianity—Catholic —General.
2. RELIGION—Christian Living—Spiritual Growth.
3. RELIGION—Christian Living—Inspirational.

eISBN: 978-1-63966-413-9
LCCN: 2026936921

Cover design: Tyler Ottinger
Cover art: *Christ the King*, by Artist, Ruth A. Stricklin, New Jerusalem Studios, Phoenix. For reproductions please visit: www.njerusalemstudios.com
Interior design: Amanda Falk
Interior art: AdobeStock

Printed in the United States of America

Contents

To the parishioners of Sacred Heart
of Jesus in Lakeville, Indiana,
and to Fr. Greg Abuya,
who served them faithfully

INTRODUCTION

Behold This Heart

Your heart is restless. It wants more than this world can give. It longs for a love that will not fail, a peace that will not pass away, a home that cannot be taken from you. You know this — perhaps you have always known it — even when you try to silence the longing with lesser things.

In the seventeenth century, Jesus revealed to St. Margaret Mary Alacoque the answer to that longing. He showed her his Sacred Heart: aflame with love, wounded by ingratitude, yearning for souls who would console him through their devotion. What she saw was not simply a vision but an invitation. Christ was opening his heart to her — and through her, to us — saying in effect: *This is what you have been seeking. This is where you belong.*

We begin here: with a heart that burns for us and a God who wants to be known not only for what he has done but for who he is. The Sacred Heart pours forth divine love — love that endures all things, love that gives without counting the cost, love that transforms those who receive it.

What follows is a thirty-three-day journey into that Sacred Heart. Thirty-three days is a customary length for Catholic devotionals, and for good reason. It requires enough time to form a habit but not so much that the commitment becomes overwhelming. It invites us to make a focused commitment that requires something of us every day, trusting that the Lord will bless our fidelity and efforts through his own generosity. We will find that devotion to the Sacred Heart leads to renewal through attentiveness, repentance, reparation, and service.

This devotional is written to guide you in the integration of reflection, prayer, practice, and deepening understanding. The first half draws you into the revelations given to Saint Margaret Mary, teaching you to contemplate the Sacred Heart as she did. The second half broadens and deepens your practice through the witness of saints who embodied this devotion, provides theological reflection on its meaning, and explores the concrete acts of mercy and prayer that sustain it. Throughout, you will encounter Scripture, the wisdom of the Church, and the daily discipline that forms you into a disciple whose heart beats with the Heart of Christ.

You can practice this devotion individually, as a family, as a parish, or as a small community of disciples. However you choose to practice it, the essential movement remains the same: You are drawing near to the Heart that has loved you from the beginning and will love you to the end.

The Sacred Heart is not an image or an idea. It is the living, burning center of divine love made flesh. Christ's heart is both human and divine, both wounded and glorified, both source and summit of all charity. To devote yourself to this Heart is to devote yourself to Christ himself.

Begin today. Give these thirty-three days to the Sacred Heart, and wait in trust for what Christ will give you in return.

Sacred Heart of Jesus, I place all my trust in you.

Part 1

The Habit of Devotion

DAY 1

Draw Near

One of his disciples,
whom Jesus loved,
was lying close to the breast of Jesus.
–JOHN 13:23

Meditation

Jesus gathered with his apostles in the Upper Room. He had spent three years with them, traveling from town to town and across the countryside as he preached, taught, and healed. He called each of the Twelve personally; in fact, he had prayed to his Father in heaven that he might choose and receive them. They were, in a very real way, a gift to him. He cherished them so much that he removed his outer garments and knelt down like a servant to wash their feet. He knew them — as they were — and he did not hesitate to give himself to them. His Father had given them to him, and he claimed them as his own. He loved them.

The apostles loved him, but not yet as they should. They were witnesses to his miracles and the first beneficiaries of his preaching. They knew the sound of his voice, the movements of his body, the cadence of his daily living. They learned how to pray by following him. They were given power to heal from him. They started to preach with his authority. Each of them had changed in those three years, and yet not so much that they were free of doubts and backsliding, failures, or even betrayal. Even here in this Upper Room, they began fighting over which of them would be the greatest, and one of them slipped out into the night to hand him over to those who would execute him. They did not give themselves fully to him.

And yet, one of the Twelve risked a special kind of intimacy. John did not keep his distance but laid his head upon the chest of his Savior. Something about the way John knew Jesus was different. Or rather, something about the way John understood Jesus' knowledge of him was different. Later, when John wrote his Gospel, he never referred to himself by name or with any first-person pronouns. Instead, he only identified himself as the "one whom Jesus loved." John had come to know himself as the "beloved disciple." For him, it was not a term of comparison, as if he were beloved and others were not. They were each beloved, and yet John seemed to grasp it with a clarity that eluded the others. For him, this was simply and essentially true — at his core, that is what he was: beloved.

At that table in the Upper Room, the disciple "whom Jesus loved" was the only one close enough to the heart of it all. In those three years with Jesus, he had learned that all the good that had come and would ever come found its source where he now placed his head. He drew near to Jesus' heart, which beat like any human heart but with a purpose unlike any other. Reclining on the breast of the Savior, the beloved disciple heard the thrum of divine charity and felt the warmth of God's love.

Lesson

Our devotion to the Sacred Heart begins with where we are willing to place ourselves. The "beloved disciple" placed himself upon his Savior's breast. That is the place of devotion.

It is a risk to do what John the Apostle did — not because we fear what Jesus will do — but because we must be willing to hear what John heard and feel what he felt. It is a risk because devotion to the Sacred Heart is about putting the love that is the heart of the world at the center of our own lives and homes. That love is not an idea, nor is it just a promise. That love took on our flesh and mingled with our blood. It is a love that gives life through death — a death that is endured and even embraced rather than avoided.

We cannot fathom the mysteries of the Sacred Heart beforehand; we can only embrace the Sacred Heart and learn from there what God's love means for us. Once we place ourselves upon the Savior's breast, we cannot dictate the outcome: that's the tremendous, glorious risk.

The steady, daily act of drawing near to the Sacred Heart of Jesus is our first and most important task. We cannot control the Sacred Heart any more than we can control the sunrise. But if we wanted to become the kind of people who make the beauty of the sunrise part of our daily life, we would and must take responsibility for putting ourselves in the right place, at the right time, day after day to witness a movement outside our own whims and preferences. We must get up early and position ourselves in view of the horizon. Just so with the devotion to the Sacred Heart: our part is to seek the heart of Jesus daily, placing ourselves near to the uncontrollable love that beats for us there.

The beloved disciple drew near to the Sacred Heart. Christ did not love him because he drew near; rather drawing near *unveiled* Christ's love for him. Our devotion begins with the basic desire and initial courage to draw near. Each day we must ask for the grace to draw near again.

Prayer (to offer in the morning, or at night for the next day)

O Sacred Heart of Jesus:
I pray that the grace you pour forth
may overcome all my sluggishness
and each of my hesitations.
Help me to respond to your call for me.
Stir up in me the courage and humility to seek you.
Give me what I need to come to you.
Amen.

Today's Mantra (*a phrase repeated in prayer; an ancient Catholic practice*)

Jesus, my love, draw me to your heart.

DAY 2

Remain

When Jesus saw his mother,
and the disciple whom he loved standing near,
he said to his mother, "Woman, behold your son!"
Then he said to the disciple, "Behold, your mother!"
–JOHN 19:26–27

Meditation

Raised up on the cross, Jesus looked back upon the way he had come. He saw the dirt and rocks across which he dragged the beams to this high point outside the city walls. That path led back to the city gates of Jerusalem, the city he had entered only five days earlier to acclaim from the crowds. Those same crowds drove him out of the city earlier that very day, pushing him to this place where he was nailed to the wood between two thieves. The path stretched out in front of him was the path of his rejection.

"Standing near," however, were those who clung to him in his sorrow. First among all stood his mother, Mary, who treasured and pondered him from his conception. She saw all things through him, with her heart. Here she remained near him in his sorrow and suffering, allowing the nails in his hands and feet to pierce her heart. Even when understanding was delayed, she clung to him. There too was that same disciple who reclined upon the breast of the Savior the night before during the Last

Supper: John, the beloved.

Where are the others? They have all kept their distance. Out of fear or shame or uncertainty, all the other disciples — even his chosen apostles — stood far off, out of sight, beyond the path he walked as the rejected Messiah. Judas handed him over, and Peter denied him; the others slept while he was in agony. They had been pulling away from him, and then they finally departed from him during his most intense suffering.

In their place Mother Mary and the beloved disciple kept company with Christ Crucified. With the other two Marys who stood with them, they bore witness to what divine love endures. The people spurned God's Son, and yet God's Son did not spurn them. He suffered their ingratitude and hardness of heart. And Mary and John wept with him.

Mary and the beloved disciple hold Jesus in their hearts because they seek a place in his Sacred Heart, which beats and bleeds for them. And in his heart they are united. When Jesus spoke from the cross, he revealed what was already true in his love: Because of him, they belong to each other. "Woman, behold, your son! … Behold, your mother!" (Jn 19:26–27). To love him is to love those whom he loves: His Sacred Heart is where communion is forged.

Calvary is not a site of consolation. And yet even amid the deepest anguish, something unexpected happens. Those who remain with Jesus in his suffering are already being made new, as one in him: "Behold!"

Mother Mary remained with her Son until his last breath and beyond. And there with her, witnessing and weeping, was the disciple "whom Jesus loved." Those who love endure suffering.

Lesson

Devotion to the Sacred Heart opens us to suffering with Jesus. None of us desires suffering for its own sake. In fact, left to our own, we would rather flee suffering than remain within its reach. But love proves itself in abiding. Whether in response to love or in pursuit of love, we discover ourselves willing to bear discomfort and even pain when we are within love's reach.

When Mary looked upon her Son on the cross, she saw his pain. His pain became hers; she felt his pain as her own. His cries became her cries; his tears, her tears. Her heart was pierced for love of him. She opened herself to suffering because she loved him. At the same time, she loved him because she suffered with him and for him.

Right there where Mary remained united to Jesus in his suffering, the beloved disciple remained with them. His love of Jesus drew him to this place of suffering, where he joined the Blessed Mother in keeping company with Jesus on the cross. The beloved disciple had drawn near to the Sacred Heart of Jesus, hearing the beat of unfailing charity and feeling the warmth of divine love. When the rest of the world had turned cruel and cold and rejected the Savior, the disciple who knew himself as beloved stayed near to the source of love that moves all things.

Remaining with Jesus is the harder part of love. He suffers ingratitude and rejection, callousness and disinterest. These scourges are held in his heart. Devotion to the Sacred Heart brings us to Jesus' suffering. Cherishing his heart entails observing and revering what Jesus suffered for our sake. We cannot do this from a distance, as if unmoved by the wounds he bears. As it was for Mary so it is for us: To truly heed his pain is to feel some part of his pain in ourselves. It means learning to mourn what is mournful, to weep over loss, to allow our own hearts to be pierced for love of him.

Prayer

O Sacred Heart of Jesus:

I pray for the grace to stay with you and to open myself to your suffering.

Help me to join your Blessed Mother in keeping company with you.

Awaken in me the will to bear the cost of love.

Give me what I need to remain with you, to allow your love to move me to your cross. Amen.

Today's Mantra

Jesus, my love, keep me close to your suffering.

DAY 3

Respond

This I command you,
to love one another.
–John 15:17

Meditation

Jesus gave his disciples a new commandment: "Love one another; even as I have loved you, that you also love one another" (Jn 13:34). His commandment was not based in words alone; his commandment was given first in action. Jesus showed his love for his disciples, beginning with the apostles in the Upper Room. Having drawn them to himself for the Last Supper, he removed his outer garments, knelt down, and washed their feet (Jn 13:1–11). He — the Master — became their servant.

First Jesus acted, then he commanded. His command was based on his action. Peter at first protested, considering himself unworthy to be served by his master. But Jesus insisted: If Peter would not allow Jesus to wash his feet, then Peter could have no part in Jesus' reign. Peter relented, and Jesus washed.

Jesus made the first move. His disciples first received. Once they had received they were commanded. The commandment pointed back to the action: to do for others what had been done for them. Friendship with Christ is born of imitation.

During his last discourses in the Upper Room, Jesus' new commandment echoed as a refrain: "This I command you, to love one another" (Jn 15:17). To love others is how disciples respond to the Lord's gift of love with gratitude. Even more, it is how disciples truly receive the Lord's gift; for what he gives is not some mere thing but rather the blessed will to give unto others.

The beloved disciple had his feet washed along with the others. He did not protest as Peter had. Instead, after he had been served, he drew "close to the breast of Jesus" (Jn 13:23). John sought the heart of the one who served him. He kept seeking that heart when it was pierced with sorrow through the passion. And from that Sacred Heart he received the new commandment: "Love one another as I have loved you."

The beloved disciple began to respond to this new commandment at the foot of the cross, when he received Jesus' mother as his own. He beheld Mary, "and from that hour the disciple took her to his own home" (Jn 19:27). John cared for her and cherished her as his own. What Jesus was to Mary by birth, John became by obedience. Listening to Jesus, the beloved disciple became a beloved son.

John was the only apostle whose life did not end in a bloody martyrdom. Instead his martyrdom was of another sort: He was a martyr in the obedience of love. To "love one another" became his daily mantra, his lifeblood. When he formed and taught others in the way of his beloved Jesus, he came back to the new commandment he had received with the others in the Upper Room. This was the same commandment that arose from Christ's action for him and the others. Jesus had first knelt down to serve them, then instructed them to kneel down to serve one another. The commandment of love was imprinted on the beloved disciple's own heart. He loved others as "beloved" with him in Christ, and he passed on to others what he himself had received: "Beloved, if God so loved us, we also ought to love one another" (1 Jn 4:11).

Lesson

Devotion to the Sacred Heart bears fruit in us for others. The heart of Jesus is the source of our salvation, and, mystery of mysteries, Jesus seeks to form our hearts after his own. In the wonder of his love he wants us not only to receive the divine love he brings but to share this love with others as if it were ours to give. He makes our own hearts sources of divine love for others. The purpose of this devotion is to be changed more and more so that in our love for Christ, our own hearts beat to the rhythm of divine charity and radiate the warmth of God's own love for the world.

Becoming Christ's "beloved" with John means receiving and giving the love that pulses from the Sacred Heart. The other apostles sealed their belovedness with the blood of their martyrdom; John sealed his belovedness with his obedience to Jesus' new commandment each and every day. Most of us are called to follow the way of Saint John, by making our small daily acts of obedience into our own form of martyrdom. Whether by life or by death, beloved disciples bear the fruit of God's love for us.

From the cross, Jesus gave John a specific call: to receive Mary as his own mother, and to become to her a beloved son. And John took her into his home. This was more than an act of kindness. It was John's first lesson in loving as Jesus loved — caring for the one Jesus cherished most.

From that moment, John was changed. He went from *being* beloved to *seeing others* as beloved. He learned to look at people the way Jesus looked at him. This is what it means to love as we have been loved.

John had once heard Jesus say, "If anyone thirst, let him come to me and drink. He who believes in me, as the Scripture has said, 'Out of his heart shall flow rivers of living water'" (Jn 7:37–38). Later, standing at the cross, John watched as "one of the soldiers pierced his side with a spear, and at once there came out blood and water" (Jn 19:34). What Jesus had promised — rivers of living water — poured from his pierced heart.

John understood. The life Jesus gives flows from his Sacred Heart into ours, and then through us to others. When we obey the commandment to "love one another as I have loved you" (Jn 15:12), we become what John became: a channel for the grace that comes from the Sacred Heart.

Prayer

O Sacred Heart of Jesus:
The wonders of your love are without end.
I pray that I may heed your commandment
to love others as you have loved me.
Help me, through my obedience to you,
to become what you call me to be for others.
Give me the grace to become a wellspring like you.
Amen.

Today's Mantra

Jesus, my love, make me a wellspring of your charity.

DAY 4

Convert

Beloved,
let us love one another;
for love is of God,
and he who loves is
born of God and knows God.
–1 JOHN 4:7

Meditation

The beloved disciple did not choose Jesus first. Rather, Jesus chose him, as he chose each of his disciples. One after another, the disciples left behind their old ways to follow Jesus and responded to his love for each of them. Like all the others, John was first loved; only afterward did he love.

John felt in his bones what he heard Jesus tell him and the others: "You did not choose me, but I chose you and appointed you that you should go and bear fruit and that your fruit should abide" (Jn 15:16). The fruit that would abide grew from Christ's love poured out for him. Because he received, the beloved disciple gave.

Failing to love is failing to know God. John knew this because he knew God's love in Christ. If he did not heed the new commandment "to love one another," then he would ultimately both neglect and forget the one who loved him first.

Jesus' mission to his disciples was that their love should

imitate his own: "As I have loved you" (Jn 13:34). In teaching them this new commandment, he called them "little children," because they had to learn both from their master's words and example. In fact they learned his words from his example.

So well did John learn from his master that he not only did what Jesus said but even taught as he taught. "Little children," John wrote to his community, "let us not love in word or speech but in deed and in truth" (1 Jn 3:18). What is to be received is first given in action, and only afterward is it grasped with words. That is the way of God's love.

"For God so loved the world that he gave his only-begotten Son," Jesus told Nicodemus — and John wrote it down (Jn 3:16). It was God's action that came first. God's action became the basis of John's own teaching to others: "In this the love of God was made manifest among us, that God sent his only-begotten Son into the world, so that we might live through him. In this is love, not that we loved God but that he loved us and sent his Son to be the expiation for our sins. Beloved, if God so loved us, we also ought to love one another" (1 Jn 4:9–11). God gives, God endures our sin and ingratitude, and God frees us to love one another. John learned the rule of the heart, first by deeds and then by words.

When the beloved disciple laid his head upon his Savior's breast, he was already responding to God's love for him. He let himself be attracted to the love that claimed him. He moved toward the Sacred Heart of Jesus, which was God's gift to him and to us: the beating heart of creation, the warmth that melts cold indifference.

The beloved disciple's first move was to draw near to God's gift. He placed himself near to the Sacred Heart of Jesus. Once there he chose to remain, even as the one who loved him entered into his passion. He endured his share in what his Savior endured, allowing his own heart to be wounded for love of

Jesus. And through that trial and suffering the beloved disciple was made new: He became for others what Christ was for him. John the Apostle was not the Savior, but he shared the salvation his Savior brought. His heart was made to be like Jesus' own. He loved them and gave his life for them, in deed and then in word.

Lesson

The devotion to the Sacred Heart of Jesus is an ongoing conversion. It means turning away from the old ways of indifference and ingratitude, of self-protection and self-concern, in a turn toward God, who loved us first in Christ. This is not done all at once but instead becomes a daily and lifelong habit of drawing near to the Sacred Heart, remaining with the Sacred Heart, and responding to the Sacred Heart.

To convert means "to go with." Whereas reverse means "to go back" and adverse means "to go against," to convert signals a harmony of movement. The movement is first God's in Christ. When we "convert," we move with him who first loved us.

The conversion to the Sacred Heart of Jesus is a movement toward the source of God's love in the world, with a willingness to share in his suffering, and for bringing the fruits of his love to others through our deeds. The repeated pattern of the devotion is what we have practiced in the past three days: draw near, remain, respond. We never get past drawing near; it is our first duty always. When we draw near to Jesus, we are to remain with him through the discomfort and sorrow that might come to us in his company as he is rejected and spurned. Remaining with him, we are given the mission to love one another as he loved us. This mission comes to us personally, and through specific and habitual actions. We practice all of this in the movements of our devotion — through prayer, meditation, and deeds. We learn the harmony of conversion through practice.

The three steps at the beginning of this devotion do not

leave us. They are repeated over and over again. We draw near, we remain, we respond. In this way we move from Christ's love, through his suffering, to loving others with him and in his love for us.

Prayer

O Sacred Heart of Jesus:
You draw me, you heal me, you transform me.
I pray that I may never tire of seeking life in you
and sharing that life with others.
Help me to move with your love.
Give me a heart devoted to you.
Amen.

Today's Mantra
Jesus, my love, I am yours.

INTERLUDE 1

The Revelations to St. Margaret Mary Alacoque

The habit of devotion to the Sacred Heart of Jesus was initiated with Saint John, the beloved disciple. He drew near to the Lord's heart, remained with the Lord in his suffering, and responded to the love of God in love for others.

Although many after John who loved Christ pondered and revered the Sacred Heart of the Savior, it was not until sixteen centuries later that devotion to the Sacred Heart passed from a private to a public devotion in the Church. That was when the Lord revealed the wonders of his heart to a young and often sickly religious sister. St. Margaret Mary Alacoque (1647–1690) was a contemplative nun of the Order of the Visitation of Holy Mary in the French village of Paray-le-Monial.

Prior to Margaret Mary, a devotion to the Sacred Heart had been developing from an earlier devotion to Christ's Holy Wounds. Devotees of the Sacred Heart included such saints as Bernard of Clairvaux (d. 1153), Bonaventure (d. 1274), Mechtilde of Helfta (d. 1298), Gertrude the Great (d. 1302), and the founder of the Visitation Order, Francis de Sales (d. 1622). What was different with Margaret Mary was that through a series of divine revelations she received, the Lord commissioned her to open this devotion to the entire Church.

The Lord appeared to Margaret Mary between December 1673 and June 1675. There are typically four apparitions counted during this period, but we will reckon them as three revelations, combining the content of two of them into one. Although it is interesting in itself to study the revelations to Saint Margaret Mary as the source of the devotion to the Sacred Heart of Jesus for the whole Church, our primary reason for meditating with these revelations is more personal in nature.

We will move slowly — day by day — with each of the three revelations over the course of nearly two weeks. Through our imaginations, our prayer, and our practice, we will seek to place ourselves into the position of Saint Margaret Mary, who was drawn into the position of John the Apostle as a beloved disciple transformed in the love of the Sacred Heart of Jesus. We will spend three days with each of the three revelations, and then a fourth day reflecting on each set of three. With each of the revelations, we will prepare ourselves for a particular form of devotion that will accompany our meditation and prayer.

The habit of devotion to the Sacred Heart of Jesus is built, day by day, through actual habits. As we progress together intentionally and attentively, we will establish the greater habit through these smaller habits. Our most important duty is to give a little time and effort each day, trusting that the Lord rewards our small acts of devotion with his great fidelity and love. By drawing near to him, remaining with him, and responding to him, the rule of his Sacred Heart becomes, little by little, the rule of our own hearts.

Part 2

Becoming the Beloved

THE FIRST REVELATION | **(DAYS 5–8)**

From the Diary of Saint Margaret Mary

Once being before the Blessed Sacrament, I felt wholly filled with this Divine Presence, and so powerfully moved by it that I forgot myself and the place which I was … [I] yielded my heart to the power of His love [and] He made me rest for a long time on His divine breast, where He uncovered to me the wonders of His love and the inexplicable secrets of His Sacred Heart, which He had hitherto kept hidden from me [but] now He opened to me for the first time.[1]

The Lord to Saint Margaret Mary

My Divine Heart is so passionately in love with men that it can no longer contain within itself the flames of its ardent charity. It must pour them out by thy means, and manifest itself to them to enrich them with its precious treasures, which contain all the graces of which they have need to be saved from perdition. I have chosen thee as an abyss of unworthiness and ignorance to accomplish so great a design, so that all may be done by Me.[2]

Act of Devotion for the Next Four Days: Receive Communion

Make a Holy Hour at least once over the next four days. Ideally, this is an hour spent before the Blessed Sacrament in Eucharistic adoration. The most important thing is to be with the Lord in the Sacrament and to strive to be as present to him as possible.

- During this time, you may elect to read short passages from Scripture, perhaps from the Gospel of

John, especially from day 13 onward. Shorter passages with greater attentiveness are better than longer passages with lesser attention.

- You may also read and reflect on the passages above from Saint Margaret Mary, giving your imagination over to the revelation of the Lord to her in the Blessed Sacrament. Consider this revelation as now given to you.
- The mantras from the first four days of our devotion may also be recited again, slowly and intentionally.

DAY 5 | **FIRST REVELATION**

Blessed Sacrament

Once being before the Blessed Sacrament, I felt wholly filled with this Divine Presence, and so powerfully moved by it that I forgot myself and the place which I was.

Meditation

Sister Margaret Mary was in the habit of adoring the Blessed Sacrament. Time and again she approached the blessed Host with prayer and reverence. Undoubtedly, she endured bouts of distraction and boredom during these periods of adoration, though she just as certainly found consolation and peace in this silent observance. The regularity of her habit prepared her for the extraordinary grace given to her for the first time on December 27, 1673.

It was the liturgical feast of St. John the Apostle. On this day the Church reveres that apostle who laid his head on the breast of the Savior, who remained with him at the cross, and who translated the Lord's love into love for others. Like John, Sister Margaret Mary drew near to the one whom she believed had claimed her in his love. Presumably, on every prior occasion when she had approached the Lord exposed on the altar, she saw nothing and heard nothing other than the ordinary sight and continuous silence of the consecrated Host. But on this feast of the beloved disciple her senses opened to receive the vision and voice of her Savior.

Margaret Mary touched the reality of the belief she had been practicing. She had come to adore the Blessed Sacrament because she believed that her Lord and her God was present there. On this day, by her own account, she "felt wholly filled with this Divine Presence." A profound change took place in her: She felt herself filled. What she believed about the Blessed Sacrament — the Lord dwells fully and completely … *here* — was communicated to her personally.

Rapt in her attention to and presence with God, her notice of herself and of her surroundings evaporated. The meaning of "who" and of "where" changed for her. Who she was became simply "the one whom God fills"; where she was became simply "with God."

In this state of presence she heard Jesus say, "I have chosen thee."

Lesson

The seemingly ordinary act of adoring the Blessed Sacrament gave rise to the extraordinary revelation of the Sacred Heart of Jesus. Margaret Mary placed herself where she believed Christ dwelt in silence under the veil of simple bread. The revelation offered to her came after she placed herself — likely innumerable times — precisely there: before the Blessed Sacrament. It mattered very much where she placed herself, just as it had mattered where the beloved disciple placed himself. Likewise it matters for us.

The approach to the Blessed Sacrament is itself an act of faith and evidence of trust. None of us approaches Jesus' veiled presence with absolute certainty, absent moments of doubt. The quality of belief is not of primary importance, though. What matters most is moving toward him, time and time again. In doing so we can trust that God will not leave our small acts of devotion unnoticed or unrewarded.

As disciples our aim in approaching Jesus in the Blessed Sacrament is not to engage in some kind of performance. Rather our aim is to be present to him. We trust that he is present to us

— even if we cannot see or hear or feel his presence in obvious ways. We grow in that trust by making ourselves more and more fully present to him in adoration. Margaret Mary eventually discovered herself "filled with this Divine Presence" after making the trek to the Blessed Sacrament time and time again. Her steps and her efforts at attentiveness constituted her openness to him. The Lord noticed and rewarded her openness with the profound gift of himself. He gave in response to her willingness to receive, and then he led her to receive even more.

Spending time adoring the Lord in the Blessed Sacrament is how we begin to open ourselves to knowing his Sacred Heart.

Prayer

O Sacred Heart of Jesus:
I pray that the grace you pour forth
may overcome all my sluggishness
and each of my hesitations.
Help me to respond to your call for me.
Stir up in me the courage and humility to seek you.
Give me what I need to come to you.
Amen.

Today's Mantra

Jesus, my love, draw me to your heart.

Act of Devotion

Make a Holy Hour at least once in these four days.

DAY 6 | **FIRST REVELATION**

Yielding and Resting

I yielded my heart to the power of His love and He made me rest for a long time on His divine breast.

Meditation

Sister Margaret Mary entered into an exchange of generosity with Jesus. He had waited for her in the Blessed Sacrament, and she came to him through repeated acts of faith and devotion. When she was prepared to receive him more fully, the Lord carried her into the intimacy of his holy presence. She yielded her heart to him, and he gave her a place to rest.

The beloved disciple's affection for the Lord became Margaret Mary's own. Just as John had reclined against the breast of his Savior at the Last Supper, so Margaret Mary placed the weight of our own sensitivities near her Savior's heart. She released herself to the rhythm of divine love pulsating in the world.

What did it mean for her to "yield her heart"? It meant giving the integrating center of her life over "to the power of His love." The heart is where the coordination of body and soul takes place, where sincerity is located, where the deepest response to the question of "Whom am I, really?" comes forth. The heart is that core where the fundamental truth of a human person is housed. This is what Margaret Mary gave over to the Lord. She entrusted herself to him.

And how did the Lord respond? He received her kindly,

even courteously. He gave her a place to rest. He did not grasp, nor did he seize. Rather he cushioned the gift of her heart and took the center of her life into his own safekeeping.

Resting upon his breast, Margaret Mary became a student of the Sacred Heart of Jesus. She listened to its sounds and she felt its warmth, its vitality. The Lord led her to "rest for a long time" so that her education would not be rushed or cursory. Might we consider the rhythm of her own heart to have adapted to the rhythm of his, just like a child's heartbeat adjusts to synchronize with that of his mother within her womb? As Margaret Mary rested, she yielded her pace and her purpose to Jesus.

Lesson

The Sacred Heart of Jesus introduces a new pace and purpose to our lives. We have become accustomed to all manner of hurry and efficiency, just as we have become all too familiar with anxieties and preoccupations. We have forgotten how to rest. And so Jesus beckons us to yield our hearts to him so that he can teach us again how to rest.

To yield our hearts to Jesus does not mean forgetting who we are or what burdens us. It means intentionally bringing what we have to him. He asks us to present our hearts to him and to entrust him with ourselves. By doing so we loosen our grip on all those many things that weigh us down. We lay the burden of our lives on him. With Margaret Mary and Saint John before her, we yield our hearts.

In return the Lord gives us a place to rest, and that "place" is nowhere other than the very center of his own life. He brings us toward his Sacred Heart into which he will receive all that we are with all that we have. He cushions us and honors us. His heart is a place to rest.

In the exchange of our generosity with his, we enter into the school of his heart. Our passions and emotions, our affections and intentions, our reasons and motivations are modulated and adjusted according to the rhythm of his heart. We cannot know in advance what that rhythm will sound like or feel like — it is not a lesson to be studied from afar or merely told of secondhand. The only way to learn the secrets of his Sacred Heart is to risk placing the center of our lives upon it, even if only a little bit at a time.

Yielding and resting are by now foreign to most of us. The rule of the heart requires us to let go of the ways we cling to control, whether that be by exerting force or exuding worries. We must learn to yield all to him; we must practice doing so. The devotion to the Sacred Heart is a meeting of hearts: ours and his. We bring our hearts to him, and he gives us his heart as our resting place.

Prayer

O Sacred Heart of Jesus:
I pray that the grace you pour forth
may overcome all my sluggishness
and each of my hesitations.
Help me to respond to your call for me.
Stir up in me the courage and humility to seek you.
Give me what I need to come to you.
Amen.

Today's Mantra

Jesus, my love, draw me to your heart.

Act of Devotion

Make a Holy Hour at least once in these four days.

DAY 7 | **FIRST REVELATION**

Secrets of Charity

He uncovered to me the wonders of His love
and the inexplicable secrets of His Sacred Heart,
which He had hitherto kept hidden from me
but now He opened to me for the first time.

Meditation

Reposed and attentive, Margaret Mary began to hear the symphony of the Sacred Heart. Removed from distractions and released from competing voices, the true and persistent notes of her Savior's love filled her mind and even her own heart. The secrets of Jesus' heart were closed off to any who were unwilling to listen or place themselves within that holy heart's aural space. But here, sharing in this intimate union, Margaret Mary received the Sacred Heart's unfiltered wonders.

What she heard she also felt. She received sound and warmth together. As her Lord told her, "My Divine Heart is so passionately in love with men that it can no longer contain within itself the flames of its ardent charity." The flesh and blood of Jesus' heart make present the very life of God, who is love. This love — the eternal giving of the Father and the Son in the union of the Holy Spirit — is then given over to human beings in unbridled passion. The charity is ardent, burning for us. There is nothing passive about the Sacred Heart: It is all will, all action, all readiness to serve and to behold.

Margaret Mary heard and felt the urgency of this divine love. As Jesus continued, "It must pour [these flames] out by thy means, and manifest itself to [human beings] to enrich them with its precious treasures, which contain all the graces of which they have need to be saved from perdition."[3] The beginning of Margaret Mary's apostolic mission is voiced here. She is to become the servant of unleashing the treasures of the Sacred Heart for the good of others. The world lives in peril, resisting and rejecting the only good that will make us well and whole. Without the treasures coming forth from this Sacred Heart, all is loss. The passion of divine love is matched by the passion of this desire to give over the graces that are necessary for salvation. Margaret Mary hears the zeal and feels the ardor of this heart.

She, a simple but devoted disciple, is the chosen instrument by which this Sacred Heart will be newly known and welcomed. "I have chosen thee," the Lord tells her, "as an abyss of unworthiness and ignorance to accomplish so great a design."[4] Margaret Mary knew and would not forget that the great good that was to be given did not come from her; it was not of her own making. Resting upon the Sacred Heart, she was told and knew in her own heart that the Sacred Heart of Jesus filled her without assistance or aid. Without the love of this heart, she would be void. But with the graces flowing from this heart, she was filled. The saving mission of the Sacred Heart would not proceed by her ingenuity but by her obedience. This was to be divine work, accomplished through human means, "so that all may be done by Me."

In this first revelation the Lord made known that divine love can no longer be hidden in his Sacred Heart. Here Jesus is the Friend, the love of the Father, who makes the tender effort to save his children. It is precisely Margaret Mary's "unworthiness and ignorance" that will serve this good end, for her humility will not obscure the unsolicited graciousness of Christ's charity.

When Margaret Mary offered her own heart to Jesus, he responded by sharing a spark of his ardent divine love with her. The fervor of that love remained with her in the form of an invisible wound in her side. On the first Friday of each month thereafter, she experienced intense heat and pain. In prayer and in passion Margaret Mary remained a student of the secrets of the Sacred Heart for six months before a second revelation.

Lesson

If we are attentive to the Sacred Heart of Jesus, we will eventually become quickened to the ardor of his charity. The paradox of resting and readying begins right away. Should we yield ourselves to his heart, Jesus will begin to disclose to us the passion with which he desires our good and the salvation of others. By resting upon his heart, we are tutored in the sweet unrest of divine charity as it beats urgently, flaming forth for us and for all.

The risk of entrusting ourselves to the Sacred Heart of Jesus is that the love we discover here means to change us. When we love — when we truly love — we begin to care about whatever our beloved cares about. In claiming us as his beloved, Jesus takes our good as his mission: He cares about our well-being, our healing, our salvation in union with him. As we allow ourselves to be claimed by him and, in return, entrust ourselves to his Sacred Heart, we grow to care about what he himself cares about.

Christ's passion will change us, when we allow it to change us. The ardor of his charity becomes in us a burning zeal. The secret of the Sacred Heart is not only that our Savior is enflamed with the desire for our salvation but also that he desires to set us ablaze with his own mission. What belongs to his Sacred Heart will, in time, come to fill our hearts completely.

Already here the notion of a "private devotion" is being dispelled. There is nothing private about the consolation that will come to us from the Sacred Heart. The graces received from him are meant to pour forth through our own means for the good of others. Our prayer and our willingness should and must adapt accordingly.

In devotion to the Sacred Heart, we dispose ourselves to receive what the Lord desires to give. Often this will exceed what we previously wanted. The attunement of Margaret Mary to the Sacred Heart is thus our model. Like her, we humbly beg to receive what the Lord wants to give. We make ourselves like "an abyss" into which he may pour what he likes. Being changed by him will cause some pain in us, as we become what we have not yet been. Touched by the burning flames of his charity, we prepare to allow his will to be accomplished through us.

Prayer

O Sacred Heart of Jesus:
I pray that the grace you pour forth
may overcome all my sluggishness
and each of my hesitations.
Help me to respond to your call for me.
Stir up in me the courage and humility to seek you.
Give me what I need to come to you.
Amen.

Today's Mantra

Jesus, my love, draw me to your heart.

Act of Devotion

Make a Holy Hour at least once in these four days.

DAY 8 | REFLECTING ON THE FIRST REVELATION

Beloved

Behold, My beloved, a precious proof of My love. I enclose in thy heart a little spark of the most ardent flame of My love, to serve thee as a heart and to consume thee till thy last moment ... henceforth thou shalt be called the well-beloved disciple of My Sacred Heart.

Meditation

It was in giving that Margaret Mary received. Jesus requested that Margaret Mary give her heart to him. She begged him to take it. He received the heart she gave him and "put into His own Adorable Heart." She saw her heart enter into his heart like a small particle into a great furnace. When Jesus withdrew her heart from his own, he gave it back to her with his own fire burning within it. What she had given to him she received back enflamed with divine charity.

There was an exchange of gifts in this renewal of the devotion to the Sacred Heart. Margaret Mary had made a gift of her own heart to the Lord. For his part, the Lord opened his Sacred Heart to Margaret Mary. The two hearts, given to each other, were not to remain separate. Rather her heart came to share in the passion and flame of his glorious heart. What she ultimately received from Jesus was a heart made new, vibrantly alive.

Jesus claimed Margaret Mary as his beloved. She came to know herself as beloved just as John the Apostle did. The most fundamental thing about her was Christ's love for her. That was what was in the core of Margaret Mary — that was her heart.

Just as Margaret Mary came to receive an identity like the beloved disciple's, so too did she come to receive an apostolic mission. She was being prepared to be "sent" on the mission of the Sacred Heart. Through her, the wonders of the Sacred Heart were to be made known and offered to the unremembering world. The sign — "the precious proof" — of this passion and ardor of divine charity would exist in her. Her passion, her ardor for the Sacred Heart, would point to the limitless passion and ardor of the Sacred Heart itself.

To become Christ's beloved is a sweet and demanding blessing. It means, at one and the same time, being known and cherished completely and totally, and relinquishing any other identity or name as primary. The well-beloved disciple of the Sacred Heart finds her meaning and truth in him alone.

Lesson

The first revelation of the Sacred Heart occurs through an initial openness and mutual giving. Jesus makes his heart available to those who seek him, but he forces his love on no one. Margaret Mary regularly sought him in the regular habit of Eucharistic adoration. Her path is one we can easily follow. In our own steps toward the Blessed Sacrament, we practice walking away from other primary ways of knowing or defining ourselves. We move instead toward him, who wills to claim us as his beloved, bestowing on us our deepest and most fundamental identity.

Understanding is less important than doing, just as grasping falls below the primacy of giving. What comes first is giving our time and attention to the Lord, as with a Holy Hour. Doing this again and again is a surer way to his Sacred Heart than wordy petitions or grandiose ambitions. Margaret Mary approached and yielded herself — her own heart — to her Savior. She did what John the Apostle had done. Both were claimed as Christ's beloved. Our call as devotees of his Sacred Heart is to do what these beloved disciples did.

Jesus is never outdone in generosity. He responds to the little we give with an overflowing abundance. We cannot predict in advance what that abundance will be like for us. Margaret Mary saw her own heart enter into Christ's heart like a small particle into a great furnace. Our devotion may bring a different vision and sense. And yet the main thing that Margaret Mary communicated was that she knew her small gift was taken into his greater gift, and was then returned to her as radically renewed, ablaze in his love. That is what we seek and can trust in: The Lord will give our hearts his own passion and love. Our part is to seek him, to yield to him, to rest in him, and to receive from him.

Prayer

O Sacred Heart of Jesus:
I pray that the grace you pour forth
    may overcome all my sluggishness
    and each of my hesitations.
Help me to respond to your call for me.
Stir up in me the courage and humility to seek you.
Give me what I need to come to you.
Amen.

Today's Mantra

Jesus, my love, draw me to your heart.

Act of Devotion

Make a Holy Hour at least once in these four days.

Part 3

The Scourge of Ingratitude

THE SECOND REVELATION | (DAYS 9–12)

From the Diary of Saint Margaret Mary

Once when the Blessed Sacrament was exposed, my soul being absorbed in extraordinary recollection, Jesus Christ, my sweet Master, presented Himself to me. He was brilliant with glory; His five wounds shone like five suns. Flames darted forth from all parts of His sacred humanity, but especially from His adorable breast, which resembled a furnace, and which, opening, displayed to me His loving and amiable Heart, the living source of these flames. … He unfolded to me the inexplicable wonders of His pure love and to what an excess He had carried it for love of men, from whom He had received only ingratitude.[5]

The Lord to Saint Margaret Mary

This is much more painful to Me than all I suffered in My Passion. If men rendered Me some return of love, I should esteem little all I have done for them, and should wish, if such could be, to suffer it over again; but they meet My eager love with coldness and rebuffs. Do you, at least, console and rejoice Me, by supplying as much as you can for their ingratitude.[6]

Act of Devotion for the Next Four Days: Confession and Communion

Over the next four days prepare yourself for sacramental confession and plan to receive holy Communion on the next Friday. Confession and Communion are two moments of the same act: We repent of our sins for Christ's sake and receive, in return, the grace of his merciful love in the Eucharist.

DAY 9 | **SECOND REVELATION**

The Wounds

Once when the Blessed Sacrament was exposed, my soul being absorbed in extraordinary recollection, Jesus Christ, my sweet Master, presented Himself to me. He was brilliant with glory; His five wounds shone like five suns. Flames darted forth from all parts of His sacred humanity, but especially from His adorable breast, which resembled a furnace, and which, opening, displayed to me His loving and amiable Heart, the living source of these flames.

Meditation

The wounds of Christ revealed his glory. During the several months after the first revelation, Margaret Mary experienced pain and felt heat in her side from where the Lord had returned her heart to her with a share of the fire of his own heart. This invisible wound stayed with her for life and was particularly intense on Fridays — the day of the Lord's passion. She had been drawn toward Christ's beauty as she laid her head upon his breast, and she came to know in her own body something of the intensity of the Lord's own passion: the passion to love that bore the passion of suffering.

Here in the second revelation, given to her in June during the octave of Corpus Christi in 1674, Margaret Mary gazed upon the glorified body of Christ. There she found the five wounds of his crucifixion shining with all the power of divine charity.

This new vision of the Lord's wounds was not separate from the suffering Margaret Mary endured by her own wound since the first revelation. She was learning to bear the intensity of Christ's love, which endures all things. Here she saw that behind the wounds was "His loving and amiable Heart, the living source of these flames," which gave his humanity its undimmed glow and radiant warmth. The wounds on his body were caused by those who pierced him from the outside. But here, in truth, these wounds were seen as revelations of divine love. Having been claimed in Christ's love and then given a share in the pain of his love in her own side, Margaret Mary encountered in Jesus what she had been discovering in her own flesh: love is passion — the passion to give light and warmth to those outside, the passion to endure the scourges of callousness and ingratitude.

The wounds and the humanity of Christ prepared Margaret Mary to see the source of the living flames: his Sacred Heart. What Christ had done for her and for us led her to see more fully who he is. Her attention passed through stages, being elevated and enlivened more and more toward the heart of love itself.

This all happened for Margaret Mary again while she adored the Blessed Sacrament. She was in "extraordinary recollection," drawing all her attention toward the divine presence of the exposed Host. From the bread to the body to the heart of Jesus, Margaret Mary's adoration went from one to the next, piercing the mystery of love.

Lesson

It seems that the Lord not only gives his graces when he wills but also when we are ready. Margaret Mary had developed the habit of adoring the Blessed Sacrament, and in time Jesus drew her toward his Sacred Heart. She continued with that habit but also learned to endure the pain of his passionate love in her own side for months and months. Again in time Jesus revealed his wounds and his humanity to her, drawing her through his glorified body toward the living flames of his Sacred Heart. We learn from this that although devotion is a response to grace given, devotion is also preparation for graces to come.

In this second week of our practice of devotion the initial enthusiasm may begin to taper. We cannot produce for ourselves inspiration or excitement, but we can commit ourselves to basic and daily habits. The regularity of our practice is the greater part of our work in this devotion. And if a day is missed, our call and our duty is to resume the next day.

The study for us entering into the movement of the second revelation is upon Christ's wounds. Where do we glimpse those wounds? No doubt in our own sins. Whereas his Sacred Heart is the source of the living flames of love and light in the world, our collective sinfulness is the source of callousness and ingratitude that neglects and rejects him. The point is not for us to collapse under the weight of our sins. Quite to the contrary, the point is to offer these to him, for he seeks to respond to us in mercy, allowing the passion of his love to undo the passion of suffering we have caused him to endure. To name and confess our sins is how his wounds become glorified for us.

The act of devotion for these days is thus to prepare and offer our sacramental confession as preparation for receiving holy Communion on the next Friday to come. This confession and Communion are two moments of the same act, by which we repent of our sins for his sake and receive, in response, the gift of his precious Body and Blood. In these sacramental acts our hearts act in favor of his Sacred Heart.

Prayer

O Sacred Heart of Jesus:
I pray for the grace to stay with you
and to open myself to your suffering.
Help me to join your Blessed Mother
in keeping company with you.
Awaken in me the will to bear the cost of love.
Give me what I need to remain with you.
Amen.

Today's Mantra

Jesus, my love, keep me close to your suffering.

Act of Devotion

Before the next Friday, offer your sacramental confession. On the next Friday, receive holy Communion.

DAY 10 | **SECOND REVELATION**

The Real Pain of the Passion

He unfolded to me the inexplicable wonders of His pure love and to what an excess He had carried it for love of men, from whom He had received only ingratitude.

This is much more painful to Me than all I suffered in My Passion. If men rendered Me some return of love, I should esteem little all I have done for them, and should wish, if such could be, to suffer it over again; but they meet My eager love with coldness and rebuffs.

Meditation

As he was standing beside the Blessed Mother at the foot of the cross, the beloved disciple heard Jesus say, "I thirst" (Jn 19:28). The reasons for his thirst seemed obvious. He was stretched out between the branches of the cross, having carried those beams through the city and up the rocky dirt road to this high point. It was the middle of the day, and the sun's rays beat down on him. Of course, he would be thirsty amid this strain and struggle, with the heat and the dust rising together. But with the Blessed Mother, John could feel the deeper reason for Jesus' thirst, which was expressed in the psalm Jesus invoked when he confessed his thirst: "I looked for pity but there was none; / and for comforters, but I found none" (Ps 69:20). Jesus was parched from the lack of compassion, and it hurt more than the nails.

Margaret Mary joined John the Apostle as witness to the Lord's passion. When Jesus disclosed the secrets of his Sacred Heart to her, she came to know the infinity of love that burns in him for his people. But as she remained there, attentive to his Sacred Heart, Jesus also disclosed the pain and grief that is absorbed in his heart. In response to his warmth the world is cold; in exchange for his mercy his people rebuff him; in consideration of his unfathomable kindness, a great many return ingratitude. The callousness that put him on the cross is now repeated in the callousness of those who ignore his sacrifice. His passionate love is turned around as a passion he endures.

The Lord did not say to Margaret Mary that he is still crucified; he was crucified once for all. In fact before he revealed to her the pain of this scourge of ingratitude, he first gave her rest upon his breast and then, later, revealed himself to her in his glory. His glory absorbs the ingratitude for him, whereas his compassion overcomes the world's lack of compassion. This new pain that the Lord showed Margaret Mary is the lack of love generated from the immense love of God for us. As Saint John himself recorded, "For God so loved the world that he gave his only-begotten Son" (Jn 3:16). The world does not love the one who loves us so.

Upon the Sacred Heart, Margaret Mary came to sense how the "pure love" that has been given over to humanity as "an excess" was neglected, ignored, rejected, and unheeded. She glimpsed the immensity of love being met by such a paucity of affection. The opening of the Sacred Heart to her was for the sake of responding to this coldness and indifference by an encounter with the ardent charity given in Jesus. Given a share in bearing the scourge of ingratitude, Margaret Mary shared his thirst.

Lesson

Contemplating Christ's suffering is a way to grow in love for him. Rather than being morose, attending to him in his passion is an act of fidelity and a pathway to gratitude. What we see in the Crucified Christ is not merely a man who has been treated unjustly and without compassion, though we do see that. More especially we see the love of God given over to us in the flesh, bearing for us our own wickedness so that we might be healed. Christ's passion is yet another exchange: our indifference and hardness of heart overcome by God's mercy and zealous affection.

When we contemplate Jesus' suffering, we need not be afraid to confess with our words, "Through my fault, through my fault, through my most grievous fault." He does not look to condemn us. Instead, just as he did for the beloved disciple and the other apostles on the first night of his rising from the dead, he offers us his peace out of the very wounds he bears. Then he breathes his Spirit upon us to give us his life anew (see Jn 20:19–22). When the apostles looked upon Jesus' wounds that night, they saw what their neglect of him and others' malice toward him had done. But when Jesus showed them these wounds, he showed them the immensity of divine love that heals those who are themselves wounded by sin.

There are certain ways in which seeing one's own sins as "crucifying Jesus" or "wounding him" are unhealthy. We can engage in hidden forms of spiritual pride in thinking this way. Let us be corrected by this second revelation, where the Lord did *not* reveal to Margaret Mary that the sinfulness of people today drives new nails into his flesh or a lance into his side. Instead he showed her that the wounds of his crucifixion brought forth the light of divine glory. He also revealed that ignoring this glory, neglecting this divine healing, and failing to respond to his compassion with acts of compassion toward others is a scandal to his

Sacred Heart. His love burns for our salvation. Denying that love is painful for him because it is ultimately painful for us.

Let our contemplation of Christ's passion lead us to a deeper contemplation of our own need for his mercy. Then we will learn to be grateful for what he has given, and always gives, for us.

Prayer

O Sacred Heart of Jesus:
I pray for the grace to stay with you
and to open myself to your suffering.
Help me to join your Blessed Mother
in keeping company with you.
Awaken in me the will to bear the cost of love.
Give me what I need to remain with you.
Amen.

Today's Mantra

Jesus, my love, keep me close to your suffering.

Act of Devotion

Before the next Friday, offer your sacramental confession. On the next Friday, receive holy Communion.

DAY 11 | **SECOND REVELATION**

The Call to Consolation

Do you, at least, console and rejoice Me, by supplying as much as you can for their ingratitude.

Meditation

In one breath, Jesus led Margaret Mary to do something for him and something for others. Her action would be one and the same. By attending to Jesus in his suffering — contemplating his passion, recognizing his sacrifice of love — Margaret Mary would both "console and rejoice" Jesus and help atone for the ingratitude of others.

This peculiar economics is so like Jesus, who once said that "as you did it to one of the least of these my brethren, you did it to me" (Mt 25:40). And again later, when addressing Saul of Tarsus, Jesus claimed the persecution rendered to his followers was done to him (see Acts 9:4–5). The suffering of rejection is Jesus', but the lack of gratitude belongs to others. Yet Jesus reckons these both together so that, in remaining with him and keeping him company, Margaret Mary would both console Jesus and help make amends for the failures of the many.

Jesus hereby continued to form Margaret Mary's heart after his own. The treasures of his Sacred Heart are not kept private, nor are they hidden behind a vault. Instead what is most fully his he pours out for others. The Son of God seeks union, just as he and the Father are one, with the Holy Spirit (see Jn 17:20–25).

For Margaret Mary to be formed to his heart meant for her to share in the fullness of his passion: the passion to love, the passion that suffers.

To be with Jesus we must be for all those whom Christ loves as his own. This is so because he makes it so. He counts what is done to him as done for others, and what is done to others as done to him. As a "well-beloved disciple of the Sacred Heart," Margaret Mary desired to stay with her beloved in his suffering and, at the same time, make up for what many others lack in their own devotion to him.

This means that any pain, discomfort, intention, or sacrifice — large or small — offered for the sake of Jesus' Sacred Heart would not only bring joy to Jesus but also help repair the broken relationship of others with him. These reparations are practices of communion: Margaret Mary making an offering for the good of others, taking as her own debt what is properly the debt others owe. This is the very way of Christ who throws his lot in with sinners though he himself is without sin. To share both the bounty and the deficit that belong to the members of Christ's body is how a well-beloved disciple of the Sacred Heart becomes further conformed to the love of God in Christ. It is a strange accounting, a peculiar economics. It is how God and not man reckons worth and balances the ledger.

Lesson

In the rule of the Sacred Heart, the Lord asks us to offer our prayers and our sacrifices for the good of others. He rejoices when we remain with him, but the fullness of his joy comes to dwell in us when we offer our devotion to him for the sake of those who need healing, especially healing from sin and callousness, coldness and ingratitude. This is how that "little spark of the most ardent flame of [his] love" is fanned into a larger and larger flame in us.

It is neither right nor just for any of us to make an accounting of the failures and ingratitude of others. We do not know the hearts of others. It is enough for us, as it was for Margaret Mary, to recognize that a great many do not respond to Christ's redeeming love by heeding his new commandment "to love one another." It is enough to know that, collectively, we offend his gift of redemption and freedom. It is enough to give our own prayers and sacrifices as but one humble offering of gratitude to him and for him. It is enough for us to trust that what Christ tells us is true: He counts our small acts both as consolation to him and reparation for the failings of others.

In contemplating the sufferings of Christ, we must thus ward off any sense of spiritual elitism because we happen to be the ones doing this discomforting work, work that others might neglect. Christ reckons it all as one. He is the one who does the work of our salvation — anything we do is merely an infinitesimal recognition of his infinite generosity. In his great generosity he allows us to bear burdens for one another, relying on one another to help heal us in him. When we make our offerings to him for the sake of others, we are being drawn into the joy of his heart. All of it is bound within the unlimited generosity of his most Sacred Heart.

Confession, offered for the good of others. Communion, offered for the good of others. Charity, offered for the good of others. Prayer and devotion, offered for the good of others. In these ways, well-beloved disciples enter into Jesus' solemn prayer: "That they may all be one; even as you, Father, are in me, and I in you, that they also may be in us, so that the world may believe that you have sent me" (Jn 17:21).

Prayer

O Sacred Heart of Jesus:
I pray for the grace to stay with you
and to open myself to your suffering.
Help me to join your Blessed Mother
in keeping company with you.
Awaken in me the will to bear the cost of love.
Give me what I need to remain with you.
Amen.

Today's Mantra

Jesus, my love, keep me close to your suffering.

Act of Devotion

Before the next Friday offer your sacramental confession. On the next Friday, receive holy Communion.

DAY 12 | **REFLECTING ON THE SECOND REVELATION**

The Dignity of the Disciple

Fear nothing, I shall be thy strength.
Listen only to what I desire of thee
to prepare thee for the accomplishment of My designs.

Meditation

Margaret Mary was called to participate in the salvation of souls. On her own, she was not capable of producing such means. But through relying on the Lord, she was equipped with the means to accomplish his designs.

In the first revelation Jesus came to Margaret Mary as she adored him in the Blessed Sacrament. He drew her closer so that she might rest upon his breast, upon his Sacred Heart. Having given her rest as she yielded her heart to him, Jesus then shared the flame of his own divine heart with her, so that a "little spark" of his ardent love might burn in her. She grew accustomed to this love for months, learning day by day how to bear such passion in herself.

In the second revelation, again while she adored the Blessed Sacrament, Jesus opened the secrets of his Sacred Heart to Margaret Mary. Held within the flames of love were also the scourges of ingratitude, the impact of the rejection of his love by so many. Margaret Mary stretched again to hold together in her devotion his blazing love and the iciness of how we have received his gift. She learned to desire with Jesus' desire and grieve over his grief. Called to remain with him in his suffering, Margaret Mary would both console her sorrowing Savior and offer reparations for the indifference of so many.

She was not a savior; she served the Savior. The generosity of the Lord exceeds all expectation, as he calls his beloved to share in all that he is and all that he has, including his mission of ushering in salvation. Jesus alone saves, but he makes his beloved disciples co-laborers in his singular work. Margaret Mary was made to share his sorrow and hasten toward his joy.

This Apostle of the Sacred Heart was, like the beloved disciple before her, prepared "to love one another" upon her Savior's breast and was commissioned in the midst of his passion. Whereas John the Apostle was first given the mission of taking the Mother of Jesus as his own, Margaret Mary was given the dual mission of making amends for others' ingratitude and keeping company with Jesus in the Blessed Sacrament. Her call had a specific shape. First the Lord asked her to receive holy Communion on the first Friday of each month. Second, she was to keep a Holy Hour with him every week between Thursday night and Friday morning. By remaining with Jesus in this weekly Holy Hour, she would both console Jesus' rejected heart and respond to the desertion of his apostles who did not keep watch with him in the Garden of Gethsemane. And by receiving holy Communion, she would communicate directly with him and offer her communion for those who deny him in the gift of the Eucharist.

The dignity of this beloved disciple flowed from being able to do something beautiful for God. The Lord need not enroll his servants in his work, but in his generosity, he made Margaret Mary a friend of his Sacred Heart and opened his mission to her. By her devotion his love would be made known again.

Lesson

We think both too much and too little of ourselves. We think too much of ourselves when we try to act as our own saviors or neglect the need for a savior, or when we try to control the lives of others as if we were their creator and redeemer. We think too little of ourselves when we conclude there is nothing we can do for others to help them, or for ourselves, or for God. The Lord knows us and gives us our true dignity. We are not saviors, but we are his instruments when we allow him to make us his friends. A marvel of salvation is that Christ wills to share the work of salvation with his friends. He opens the sorrow and the joy of these sacred healings with us.

It is tempting at this point to separate ourselves from the call to Saint Margaret Mary. She is the "Apostle of the Sacred Heart." She is the one who received the burning furnace of his love. She is the one tasked with keeping these particular devotions, and ultimately of setting the foundation for renewal by the Sacred Heart across the Church. She — and not we.

But what is given through one disciple is intended for all. In this case, not only the fruits of Margaret Mary's devotion have come to us down the years, but also the habits of her devotion are given to us. We cannot produce or elicit revelations like the ones she received. What we can do is take up her practices in fidelity to Christ, imitating the same obedience she herself exercised. She encountered the Sacred Heart of Jesus and then began to fulfill the call she received there. We may practice fulfilling that call and so grow in union with the same Sacred Heart she encountered. The Sacred Heart of Jesus is for her and for us, and through us for others.

The act of devotion for these four days has been twofold: to make a confession and to receive Communion. To do these things is already itself a sign of our fidelity and devotion to the Sacred Heart of Jesus. The Lord cherishes our obedience to him and counts such acts as both consoling to him and healing for others.

If, by the end of our thirty-three-day devotion, we desire to make this devotion an ongoing and regular habit, we would do well to return to these two acts of devotion that the Lord gave to Margaret Mary through the second revelation. The first is to receive holy Communion on the first Friday of every month, and the second is to keep a Holy Hour (preferably before the Blessed Sacrament) every week, ideally on the night between Thursday and Friday in response to his abandonment in the Garden of Gethsemane.

Prayer

O Sacred Heart of Jesus:
I pray for the grace to stay with you
and to open myself to your suffering.
Help me to join your Blessed Mother
in keeping company with you.
Awaken in me the will to bear the cost of love.
Give me what I need to remain with you.
Amen.

Today's Mantra

Jesus, my love, keep me close to your suffering.

Act of Devotion

Before the next Friday, offer your sacramental confession. On the next Friday, receive holy Communion.

Part 4

The Life of the Church

THE THIRD REVELATION | (DAYS 13–16)

The Lord to Saint Margaret Mary

Behold this Heart which has so loved men that it has spared nothing, even to exhausting and consuming itself, in order to testify its love. In return, I receive from the greater part only ingratitude, by their irreverence and sacrilege, and by the coldness and contempt they have for Me in this sacrament of love. … It is for this reason I ask thee that the first Friday after the Octave of the Blessed Sacrament be appropriated to a special feast, to honor My Heart by communicating on that day, and making reparation for the indignity that it has received. And I promise that My Heart shall dilate to pour out abundantly the influences of its love on all that will render it this honor or procure its being rendered.[7]

From the Diary of Saint Margaret Mary

Our Divine Lord assured me that He takes a singular pleasure in being honored under the figure of His Heart of flesh, the image of which He wishes to be exposed in public in order to touch the unfeeling hearts of men. He promised that He would pour out in abundance into the hearts of all those who would honor His Heart all the gifts with which It is filled, and that everywhere this image is exposed and honored, it would draw down all kinds of blessings.[8]

Act of Devotion for the Next Four Days: Enthrone the Image of the Sacred Heart

Over the next four days, prepare to enthrone an image of the Sacred Heart in your home. Obtain an image — a picture or statue — of the Sacred Heart. Choose a place of honor in your home where the image will be displayed: a table, mantelpiece, or prominent wall. If possible, have the image blessed by a priest beforehand.

By the end of these four days, place the image in this location. Gather your household and pray together the act of consecration found at the end of this book, acknowledging Christ as the true heart of your home. This is not superstition but a visible sign of an invisible reality: Your home has been given over to the reign of the Sacred Heart.

DAY 13 | THIRD REVELATION

Absorbing and Giving

Behold this Heart which has so loved men that it has spared nothing, even to exhausting and consuming itself, in order to testify its love. In return, I receive from the greater part only ingratitude, by their irreverence and sacrilege, and by the coldness and contempt they have for Me in this sacrament of love.

Meditation

The third and final revelation to Saint Margaret Mary occurred on June 16, 1675, again during the octave of Corpus Christi, the eight days following the feast. She was kneeling at the choir-gate, praying before the tabernacle, when the Lord came to her this final time. Through this revelation the Lord moved from granting Margaret Mary personal favors to investing her with a public mission for the good of the Church.

The Lord offers again his Sacred Heart for Margaret Mary to behold in reverence and with devotion. This is the heart that brings forth abundant, unmerited love for the world. The greatness of divine love is made present in this heart. The evidence of this love lies in the great lengths to which Jesus has gone for our redemption, loving us even to death, death on the cross. His Passion makes visible God's love.

But this same Sacred Heart, which presents the limitlessness of divine love, has received in response ingratitude, irreverence, even sacrilege. Not just to ignore but even to spurn, mock, and disdain the love given to us in the Son is scandalous to his heart. This is to our peril. His heart is the site of the clash between the warmth of divine love and the coldness of human contempt.

And yet still, enduring through the continual rejection and persistent resistance to this gift of love, the Lord remains faithful in bringing about the salvation of his people, healing them of their indifference and transforming them into a people after his own heart. In presenting his Sacred Heart again to Margaret Mary, the Lord offered for her contemplation and acceptance this entire mystery: love offered, love spurned, love renewed again and again, world without end.

The Sacred Heart of Jesus is a heart of love, which absorbs pain and returns affection. Margaret Mary came to know that the Lord does not protect his heart but keeps it open despite our disregard for his love. Beholding this heart meant, for Margaret Mary, seeing and revering the seriousness, the resilience, and the indefatigability of divine love. When faced with coldness and contempt, the Savior does not respond in kind. The divine response revealed by his Sacred Heart is to meet coldness with more warmth, contempt with more affection. The gift of the Sacred Heart is a gift to a world that has, by and large, rejected the Savior. But by his heart Jesus appeals again and again for a response of love, for our good.

Lesson

We should allow ourselves to be surprised again — disarmed even — by the persistence of divine love. Before the tabernacle or even the Blessed Sacrament itself, we encounter the love of God in the Son that endures through all generations, in season and out of season, come what may. He remains, though we stray. Heeding his command to "Behold this Heart" requires us to place ourselves over and over again in the humble position of allowing his endless love, his untiring fidelity, to overawe us.

By this third and final revelation, the Lord would give to Margaret Mary her specific mission for the good of the Church. But first he returned her to the source of all renewal and goodness: his Sacred Heart. Like her, we are called to locate the missions the Lord gives to each of us in his gift of love. Adoring his Sacred Heart may become our perpetual beginning.

In response to the ways in which we and others have neglected Christ's love or taken him for granted, we are called here to observe again the outpouring of his love. His affection for us is not deserved before it is given; it is given in advance. To tutor us in a response of affection for God's gift of love for us, we may enthrone an image of the Sacred Heart of Jesus in our homes. To see the image of this heart regularly, in our comings and goings and in the midst of domestic life, reminds us that this Sacred Heart is the source of our life, the furnace that warms our cool indifference, the gift that endures for us through pain and sorrow.

This image shows us the heart that absorbs the pain we inflict, that gives affection perpetually. The Sacred Heart will warm us if we let it. By this love we are healed.

Prayer

O Sacred Heart of Jesus:
The wonders of your love are without end.
I pray that I may heed your commandment
to love others as you have loved me.
Help me, through my obedience to you,
to become what you call me to be for others.
Give me the grace to become like you.
Amen.

Today's Mantra

Jesus, my love, make me a wellspring of your charity.

Act of Devotion

In these four days dedicated to the third and final revelation, work on enthroning an image of the Sacred Heart of Jesus in your home. Establish too a regular act of devotion through this image, whether it be through a small prayer you offer before this image each morning or evening, the Sign of the Cross that you pause to make whenever you pass this image, or an act of reverence like kissing or touching the image you make at particular moments in the day.

DAY 14 | **THIRD REVELATION**

For the Whole Body

It is for this reason I ask thee that the first Friday after the Octave of the Blessed Sacrament be appropriated to a special feast, to honor My Heart by communicating on that day, and making reparation for the indignity that it has received.

Meditation

Through the devotion of Margaret Mary, Christ willed to send the treasures of the Sacred Heart to the whole Church. The mission of this well-beloved disciple of the Sacred Heart was personal, but it was not private. As with all the graces that flow to the Church from its Head, the ardent charity of the Sacred Heart would not be contained in one heart alone. By the rule of Christ, what was given first to this one member of his Body was meant for the whole Body.

The Lord channels his extraordinary mercy through ordinary means. First there was the regularity of prayer and adoration that Margaret Mary herself observed. Then there was the enkindling of her ordinary human heart with a spark of divine love. Finally, there would be the communication of this fidelity and devotion through the liturgical life of the Church.

Jesus did not send this apostle of his Sacred Heart to crown this renewed devotion with an otherworldly practice. Rather, as is his custom, he humbled himself and sent the fire of his divine love into the ordinary rhythm of the Church's liturgical calendar. By the institution and observance of this new feast day, Jesus willed to introduce anew the rhythmic beating of his own heart to the ongoing life of the Church. And along with the beating of his divine charity, the Savior deemed to transfuse to the Church the warmth of God's love.

Here again two purposes are united in one action. On the one hand, the feast would honor the Sacred Heart, through which God's love for the world flows. On the other hand, lifting up this heart by liturgical observance would serve as an act of reparation — a communal act of penance — for the abuses against the gift of divine love. Illness would thus be remediated through the practice of good health; contempt and ingratitude would be undone through affection and devotion. What Margaret Mary herself first witnessed and experienced in the Sacred Heart would, through the institution of a new feast, be translated into a mystery revealed at the heart of the Church.

The ultimate end of this devotion was, thus, to warm the Church with Christ's divine love. Through this young religious sister — meek and humble of heart — the Lord sought to drive out what is old and stale in the Church with the fire of love pouring forth from his own heart. Upon this third revelation, in which the Lord proclaimed his desire for the institution of a feast, this devotion to the Sacred Heart passed into the Church's common and universal practice.

Nearly two centuries later, in 1865, Pope Pius IX instituted the solemnity of the Sacred Heart of Jesus for the universal Church. This feast would be observed on the second Friday after Trinity Sunday, which is also the Friday immediately following the feast of the Most Holy Body and Blood of Jesus (Corpus Christi) in the United States. The Church's liturgical calendar thus follows the path of the revelation of the Sacred Heart: from the triune love of God, through the Body and

Blood of Jesus, by the union of our hearts with our Savior's.

Lesson

In the life of the Church, the good of one is the good of all, and the graces of the whole are given for the benefit of each member. What we cultivate personally as a devotion is, ultimately, meant to be offered for the benefit of others. Indeed, devotion to the Sacred Heart is a work of the whole Church.

By the stages of his revelation, Jesus has prepared his well-beloved disciples to share in his love and in his work. In our observance, we absorb with him the indignity he receives as we give him honor and reverence. As members of the Church, his Body, he leads us to learn this movement in our own hearts. Ultimately, however, our personal devotions are to be gathered up into the communal devotion of the Church.

There is no Church without the members. This means that nothing happens in the Church that does not happen in and for Christ's disciples. The Church does not exist in the abstract but rather in flesh and blood, in persons claimed as Christ's own, persons joined together in the communion of his love. The public devotion to the Sacred Heart of Jesus in the Church's liturgical life at once pronounces and provides for the personal devotion of each one of us. In cultivating the devotion to the Sacred Heart personally and communally, we move toward answering Jesus' prayer to his Father "that they may all be one" (Jn 17:21).

Prayer

O Sacred Heart of Jesus:
The wonders of your love are without end.
I pray that I may heed your commandment
to love others as you have loved me.
Help me, through my obedience to you,
to become what you call me to be for others.
Give me the grace to become like you.
Amen.

Today's Mantra

Jesus, my love, make me a wellspring of your charity.

Act of Devotion

Acts of devotion to increase our joy in and gratitude for the Sacred Heart of Jesus are not only good for us personally but also for one another as members of Christ's one Body. In these four days dedicated to the third and final revelation, work on enthroning an image of the Sacred Heart of Jesus in your home. Establish, too, a regular act of devotion through this image, whether it be through a small prayer you offer before this image each morning or evening, the Sign of the Cross that you pause to make whenever you pass this image, or an act of reverence like kissing or touching the image you make at particular moments in the day.

DAY 15 | **THIRD REVELATION**

The Sure Hope of His Promises

And I promise that My Heart shall dilate to pour out abundantly the influences of its love on all that will render it this honor or procure its being rendered.

Our Divine Lord assured me that He takes a singular pleasure in being honored under the figure of His Heart of flesh, the image of which He wishes to be exposed in public in order to touch the unfeeling hearts of men. He promised that He would pour out in abundance into the hearts of all those who would honor His Heart all the gifts with which It is filled, and that everywhere this image is exposed and honored, it would draw down all kinds of blessings.

Meditation

The Sacred Heart of Jesus is available. Margaret Mary learned this through the course of three revelations. This most precious treasure is neither hidden nor reserved. Any who seek, find. Even more, as the Lord told his well-beloved disciple in this final revelation, the more we are willing to receive, the more we shall be given. It is not a choice between restraint or liberality on the part of the Lord; rather, the degree of goodness depends on the desire of the one who seeks. The Sacred Heart of Jesus opens ever wider in pouring out divine love the more people honor this heart. This has nothing to do with reward; it is all about capacity and receptivity.

The Lord drew Margaret Mary to himself with cords of tenderness and the promise of rest. She made her home upon his breast, yielding herself to the rhythm and warmth of the Sacred Heart. She then received a share of his love in her own heart, love that burned within her in a pain that was real. She continued returning to honor the one she loved, adoring the Blessed Sacrament and drawing near to him in the tabernacle. Her honor for the Lord increased, and in response to her openness and desire to be near him, the Lord continued to pour out more of his love to her through his Sacred Heart. Jesus drew Margaret Mary into a mission to help renew the Church through a devotion patterned on the one she herself had fostered. By her obedience to this call, the abundant influences of divine charity flowed to the whole Church.

To keep her heart fixed on Jesus, Margaret Mary placed her gaze and her intention on the Sacred Heart. The image of this heart had been impressed in her memory and imprinted into her mind. But to bring this devotion to those who had not received the visions she received, the externalization of this image was necessary. And so the Lord promised her that all who expose and revere the image of his Sacred Heart in public — whether in homes or in parishes or elsewhere — would find the graces of his heart blessing them and those who joined them in reverence.

The Lord was eager to share his blessings. He told Margaret Mary that he would count honor rendered to the image of his Sacred Heart as true honor rendered to him. He pledged to respond generously to the openness and desire of those who sought him through their reverence. As Margaret Mary herself knew well, the Lord would not be outdone in generosity, nor would he withhold anything for those who sought him earnestly.

Lesson

The Lord is trustworthy. Believing his promises is to trust him. The entire record of God's actions through salvation history — up to and including the life, death, and Resurrection of Jesus — reveal that God is faithful to his promises. When offered the promises of Jesus through his Sacred Heart, what we are asked to give is our trust in the one who makes the promises. The promises are not tested in advance of trust; instead, trust precedes the fulfillment of the promises.

When the Lord promises, therefore, that the gifts of his Sacred Heart would be poured out to all those who venerate the very image of his heart, he is beckoning us — who would be his beloved disciples — to trust him. The more we open ourselves to him and desire what he promises, the more generous we will find him toward us. He asks for little and offers much.

The visions entrusted to Margaret Mary are not likely to be our own. But the repetition of her unique experience is not the necessary thing. What is necessary is to receive the love that is offered us in Christ, to allow ourselves to be filled and changed by this love, and to respond to it in gratitude and charity. In place of the visions, the Lord offers us the image of his heart. By presenting this image in our homes and parishes, our schools and workplaces, we place his Sacred Heart in the thick of our lives and open a way for others to discover this love poured out for them, too.

The image is an invitation to honor and reverence, which may then be rendered to this heart through moments of silent meditation, brief prayers for one's own needs and the needs of others, a simple expression of gratitude at times through the day, bowing or making the Sign of the Cross when passing by. Moreover, dedicating a short period of the day, each day, to venerating the image of his Sacred Heart forms in us the openness and desire to receive more and more of what the Lord is eager to give us.

Prayer

O Sacred Heart of Jesus:
The wonders of your love are without end.
I pray that I may heed your commandment
to love others as you have loved me.
Help me, through my obedience to you,
to become what you call me to be for others.
Give me the grace to become like you.
Amen.

Today's Mantra

Jesus, my love, make me a wellspring of your charity.

Act of Devotion

In these four days dedicated to the third and final revelation, work on enthroning an image of the Sacred Heart of Jesus in your home. Establish, too, a regular act of devotion through this image, whether it be through a small prayer you offer before this image each morning or evening, the Sign of the Cross that you pause to make whenever you pass this image, or an act of reverence like kissing or touching the image you make at particular moments in the day.

DAY 16 | REFLECTING ON THE THIRD REVELATION

Into Communion

I do not pray for these only, but also for those who believe in me through their word, that they may all be one; even as you, Father, are in me, and I in you, that they also may be in us, so that the world may believe that you have sent me.

–JOHN 17:20

He has given me to know that His Sacred Heart is the Holy of holies, the sanctuary of love; that He wishes to be known in our day as the Mediator between God and man, for He is all-powerful to restore us peace, by turning from us the chastisements our sins deserve, and to obtain mercy for us.

Meditation

In the Sacred Heart of Jesus, the needs of the world meet the Father's love. This heart beats in this world and, by Christ's Ascension, has returned to the Father from whom the Son came. Margaret Mary observed this heart as the holy of holies. Indeed, the Sacred Heart is a sanctuary of love, because the presence of God comes to dwell among us and calls us to worship. The prayer of Jesus in this world was for this union between God and us. By his Sacred Heart he gives the space for the fulfillment of that prayer.

In her devotion, Margaret Mary came to know and trust in the great exchange that occurs within the Sacred Heart of Jesus. This heart absorbs indignities, contempt, and sin, but returns mercy. From whatever condition we might find ourselves, even mired in our own sin or complicit in the sin of others, the Sacred Heart opens for us a way to divine love. Christ opens everything to us so that we bring everything to him.

By his Incarnation the Son of God plunged into communion with us. By his passion he endured our resistance to his company. By his Resurrection he rose from beneath our sinfulness. By his Ascension he blazed our path into communion with the Father. Margaret Mary discovered that we enter into the entire mystery of the Son of God when we enter into devotion to his Sacred Heart. She learned to seek the Savior who claims us as we are and carries us to the Father.

Lesson

The image of the Sacred Heart is not merely an image but a sign of the thing itself. The image is not the reality, but it points us to the reality. By meditating on the image, we practice directing our attention and affections toward Jesus' Sacred Heart.

And yet the Sacred Heart is an image still. It is the reality of the love of God poured into the world, and it is a sign of that love. It points to what it makes present. For us the duty is to receive what is signified and accept what is offered.

What is signified and offered? The entire mystery of the Son's descent to our humanity and his offering of our humanity to the Father. There is action and drama pulsing through his heart — it is not a static or dormant thing. Gazing upon his heart with devotion is at once the command and the invitation to reckon with the active love of God for us. God has acted; the Son is the definitive divine action. And when we begin to feel awe before this heart, we will have begun to know this inconceivable love in our own hearts.

Our hearts become hearts for others when we know the love of the Sacred Heart.

Prayer

O Sacred Heart of Jesus:
The wonders of your love are without end.
I pray that I may heed your commandment
to love others as you have loved me.
Help me, through my obedience to you,
to become what you call me to be for others.
Give me the grace to become like you.
Amen.

Today's Mantra

Jesus, my love, make me a wellspring of your charity.

Act of Devotion

Here at the conclusion of these four days dedicated to the third and final revelation, the work of enthroning an image of the Sacred Heart of Jesus in your home should be complete. It is now time to meditate on this heart. Exercise the regular act of devotion to this image you have been establishing, whether that be through a small prayer you offer before this image each morning or evening, the Sign of the Cross that you pause to make whenever you pass by, or an act of reverence you make, like kissing or touching the image, at particular moments in the day.

DAY 17 | **MIDWAY**

The Heart of the Matter

He made me rest for a long time.[9]

We are fostering a devotion to the Sacred Heart of Jesus. A devotion is an act of honor and affection. A devotion is not a set of tasks to complete. And so, to preserve us from moving too diligently through a series of days that might feel like a task list, we rest here in the middle of our thirty-three days. In our rest we give thanks both for what has been and for what is to come.

Over the past sixteen days, we have placed ourselves before the Sacred Heart of Jesus, first imaginatively alongside John the Apostle and then contemplatively through the revelations to Saint Margaret Mary. We have matched our study with daily prayers, simple mantras, and repeated exercises of devotion. We may have faltered some days and forgotten to observe what we intended. Yet we give thanks to the Lord for guiding us this far. We trust that he receives our desire and the work of our longing with generosity and graciousness.

Over the next sixteen days, we will move in different ways. First we will journey through three separate three-day cycles of devotion, meditation on a saint, and theological reflection to enter more fully with body, heart, and mind into the warmth and light of the Sacred Heart. We will then spend another three days both praying and contemplating the Litany of the Sacred Heart. Finally, on our last four days, we will immerse ourselves in the promises

Jesus makes to those who venerate his Sacred Heart. Day by day, we allow ourselves to be formed by Jesus as his beloved.

Today is reserved for simply enjoying the call to become friends of the Sacred Heart. We give thanks to the Lord for what he has begun in us. We look forward with hope for what he will do for us. And we rest in the knowledge that his love for us is without end.

Prayer

Today we offer the Prayer of Thanksgiving and Praise to the Sacred Heart:

Lord Jesus,
You deserve all honor and praise,
because your love is perfect and your heart sublime.
My heart is filled to overflowing with gratitude
for the many blessings and graces
you have bestowed upon me
and those whom I love.

Forever undeserving, may I always be attentive
and never take for granted
the gifts of mercy and love
that flow so freely and generously
from your Sacred Heart.
Heart of Jesus, I adore you.
Heart of Jesus, I praise you.
Heart of Jesus, I thank you.
Heart of Jesus, I love you forever and always.
Amen.

INTERLUDE 2 | **HEART, HASTE, AND HOPE**

For the next nine days, we will move through three, three-day cycles. On the first day of each cycle, we will introduce and reflect on a particular devotional practice. On the second day, we will contemplate a particular saint who exercised a devotion to the Sacred Heart. Then on the third day, we will deepen our understanding of Christ by studying together some facet of the theology of the Sacred Heart. These three cycles of days will form us in our heart, our haste, and our hope in response to the Sacred Heart. The next nine days will proceed as follows:

First Cycle: Heart
Day 18. *Devotion*: Morning Offering through the Immaculate Heart of Mary
Day 19. *Saint*: Louis de Montfort
Day 20. *Theology*: On the Heart

Second Cycle: Haste
Day 21. *Devotion*: Work of Mercy
Day 22. *Saint*: Faustina Kowalska
Day 23. *Theology*: On Beholding

Third Cycle: Hope
Day 24. *Devotion*: Novena to the Sacred Heart
Day 25. *Saint*: Padre Pio of Pietrelcina
Day 26. *Theology*: On the Decision

Part 5
Heart

DAY 18 | **DEVOTION**

Morning Offering Through the Immaculate Heart of Mary

Let it be to me according to your word.
—LUKE 1:38

Salvation dawned in the Annunciation to Mary. The fullness of divine generosity was met by the fullness of human freedom. What was old would become new, what was dark would become light, what was stale would become fresh.

The Word became Flesh in Mary. From the moment the angel spoke to her, Mary pondered the movement and mystery of God. In his infancy narrative, Saint Luke presents this pondering as Mary's first defining characteristic. She opens her heart to the message of the angel, to the proclamation of the shepherds, to the prophecy of Simeon, and to the perplexing words and actions of Jesus in the Temple. Never hiding or protecting her heart, Mary makes her heart available, even vulnerable. She allows herself to be continually shaped to the love of God in Christ, her Son.

Mary is the first devotee of the Sacred Heart of Jesus. Her heart becomes like his. She is Immaculate: preserved from sin, freed for obedience, wholly committed to the demands and delights of divine love. In our devotion to the Sacred Heart, we beg that our hearts may, like Mary's, be conformed to Christ's.

The heart of Mary leads to the heart of Christ, and his heart is offered through hers. By invoking the Immaculate Heart of Mary, we accept Christ's mother as our mother and ask her to show us how to open our hearts to her Son. Openness to Jesus is a daily offering.

For each of the next three days, make a morning offering to the Sacred Heart of Jesus through the Immaculate Heart of Mary. Perhaps you will choose to continue making this offering each morning thereafter. This is a way to set the intention of each day toward joining in Christ's saving mission, offering reparation for sins, and seeking the unity of all Christians. This offering changes the meaning of our days under the guidance of the Blessed Mother.

Morning Offering (Days 18–20)

O Jesus, through the Immaculate Heart of Mary,
I offer you my prayers, works, joys, and sufferings of this day in union with
the Holy Sacrifice of the Mass throughout the world.
I offer them for all the intentions of your Sacred Heart:
for the salvation of souls, the reparation of sins, the reunion of all Christians.
I offer them for the intentions of our bishops and all apostles of prayer, and in particular, for those recommended by our Holy Father this month.
Amen.

DAY 19 | **SAINT**

Louis de Montfort

Christian, by Mary's Heart, we love the Heart of Jesus.
–Hymn 40

In the decades immediately following the revelations to Saint Margaret Mary Alacoque, the devotion to the Sacred Heart began to blossom in the hearts of many saints, through whom the love of the heart of Jesus spread ever more widely. Known above all as the great apostle of Marian devotion, St. Louis de Montfort was also a fervent lover of the Sacred Heart and helped carry this devotion into new corners of the Church. In the congregation he founded, the Missionaries of Mary, he encouraged love for the heart of Jesus through sacred images and, even more deeply, through his words of prayer and song.

Saint Louis poured his love for the heart of Jesus into verse — hundreds of lines that flow with tenderness and adoration. His devotion to Mary was never apart from his devotion to Christ; in fact, Mary was the sure path that led him most deeply into the mystery of divine love. In one of his hymns, he sings:

> Heart of my God, glorious Heart,
> It is only You whom I adore,
> But in adoring You, I honor
> The Heart of the Queen of Heaven.

For Saint Louis, the heart of Jesus and the heart of Mary cannot be separated. He writes:

> From the blood of Mary's Heart, all aflame,
> The Heart of Jesus had been formed.

And again, he declares:

> In praising this adorable Heart
> I praise in due proportion
> The Heart of His admirable Mother,
> So close is their union.[10]

Through these words of praise, Saint Louis reveals how his devotion to the Sacred Heart is born of his love of Mary. Jesus' precious heart first radiates within Mary. To love her, therefore, is to be drawn toward the fire of her Son's merciful love. Mary's heart shares in her Son's warmth and becomes for others a guide to his Sacred Heart. Mary's Son is the Son of God, in whom divine tenderness embraces the flesh and blood of our humanity.

Like Saint Margaret Mary, Saint Louis discovers that this love calls for more than admiration — it calls for response. Love, adoration, consecration, and reparation are, for Louis, the four movements of a heart united to Christ. In company with Mary's heart, the Sacred Heart of Jesus burns with compassion for sinners and beats urgently for our salvation. To dwell in Christ's Heart is to share his zeal, his sorrow, his joy. By devotion to Mary, Saint Louis beckons us to the Blessed Mother, who in turn unites us to her Son: heart to heart.

Morning Offering (Days 18–20)

O Jesus, through the Immaculate Heart of Mary,
I offer you my prayers, works, joys, and sufferings of this day in union with
the Holy Sacrifice of the Mass throughout the world.
I offer them for all the intentions of your Sacred Heart:
for the salvation of souls, the reparation of sins, the reunion of all Christians.
I offer them for the intentions of our bishops and all apostles of prayer, and in particular, for those recommended by our Holy Father this month.
Amen.

DAY 20 | **THEOLOGY**

On the Heart

Only the heart is capable of setting our other powers and passions, and our entire person, in a stance of reverence and loving obedience before the Lord.
–Pope Francis, *Dilexit Nos*, no. 27

Animals do not have hearts in the way that humans do. Yes, like us, animals have a physical organ that pumps blood through the body. But what we mean by the human heart is not reducible to this physiological reality. When we speak of the human heart, we mean — and have always meant — the whole of a person's attitudes, the core of a person's existence, the seat of a person's ultimate meaning.

The heart of Jesus is a human heart, and we need to explore the full range of the human heart's meaning to begin to grasp the meaning of the heart of Christ. And yet even that range is not enough. What gives unity to Jesus' heart is, as the Jesuit theologian Karl Rahner put it, "not merely the human love of Christ ... but the divine-human love, that is the divine love of the eternal Word Himself, which ... is incarnate in the human love of Christ."[11]

This heart is the seat of divine love in the world, divine love that has been communicated through human love and that is the fundamental motivation, the genuine decision of Jesus Christ for the salvation of the world. In and through this heart, divine love has been translated into human life, human action, human sacrifice. His physical heart is flesh full of blood. That singular heart is a singular image of the Incarnation: "And the Word became flesh and dwelt among us. For God so loved the world that he gave his only-begotten Son" (Jn 1:14; 3:16).

The Sacred Heart of Jesus is not reducible to the flesh and blood of this physical heart, but Jesus' physical heart is nonetheless the symbol of the Sacred Heart. His flesh is the site of the Word's dwelling in creation. His blood is divine love coursing through human flesh. His heart is the union of flesh and blood — the sign of the union of humanity and divinity — and what God has joined, no one may separate (see Mt 19:6).

The Lord revealed his human heart to St. Margaret Mary Alacoque. It is not the mere heart muscle of a bodily organ but rather the whole being, the entire reality of Jesus Christ. In revealing his Sacred Heart, Jesus reveals who he is most deeply: that is, the suffering love that has been poured out for the life of the world.

This love is total and unreserved. His heart is the full expression of his self-giving, the complete dedication of his life in one single movement of love. To give his heart is to give himself entirely. In this gift, the mystery of the Incarnation becomes intimate and personal, inviting each of us to dwell in the heart of love himself.

Morning Offering (Days 18–20)

O Jesus, through the Immaculate Heart of Mary,
I offer you my prayers, works, joys, and sufferings of this day in union with
the Holy Sacrifice of the Mass throughout the world.
I offer them for all the intentions of your Sacred Heart:
for the salvation of souls, the reparation of sins, the reunion of all Christians.
I offer them for the intentions of our bishops and all apostles of prayer, and in particular, for those recommended by our Holy Father this month.
Amen.

Part 6

Haste

DAY 21 | **DEVOTION**

Work of Mercy

As you did it to one of the least of these
my brethren, you did it to me.
–MATTHEW 25:40

The Sacred Heart of Jesus is not a static symbol but a living reality — a heart that beats with active love. When we draw near to this heart, when we rest upon it and learn its rhythm, we discover that divine love is not merely feeling but action. Love does not turn away from need but bends down to meet it. Love moves toward suffering. This is mercy: love that acts in response to suffering.

The devotion to the Sacred Heart naturally flows into the practice of mercy. As we have learned through the revelations of Saint Margaret Mary, the Sacred Heart absorbs indignities, contempt, and sin, but returns mercy. This great exchange — taking in our coldness and pouring out warmth, receiving our hardness and giving tenderness — is the very pattern that Christ wishes to establish in our own hearts. When our hearts begin to beat in rhythm with his, we too become agents of this merciful exchange.

The Lord told Saint Margaret Mary, "Do you, at least, console and rejoice Me, by supplying as much as you can for their ingratitude."[12] But how do we console the heart of Jesus? How do we help repair the ingratitude and coldness of the world?

We do so not only through prayer and adoration, though these are essential, but also through deeds of mercy. When we feed the hungry, give drink to the thirsty, clothe the naked, shelter the homeless, visit the sick and imprisoned — when we comfort the sorrowful, instruct the ignorant, counsel the doubtful, bear wrongs patiently, pray for the living and the dead — we are doing what Jesus himself has done. We are allowing his compassion to overcome callousness through us.

The Works of Mercy are not separate from our devotion to the Sacred Heart; they are its visible flame. They are how the "little spark" of divine love that burns within us blazes forth for others to see and feel. The beloved disciple learned this at the foot of the cross when he received Mary as his own mother. His first act of responding to Christ's love was a concrete work of mercy: taking Mary into his home and caring for her. John's love was not abstract — it was done with his hands and feet, through a home he offered, by the daily acts of service he rendered.

So too for us. The warmth we receive from the Sacred Heart is meant to radiate outward. The compassion that melts our own cold hearts must flow through us to warm others, especially those who are victims of the frigid indifference of the undisturbed masses. This is the peculiar economics of the kingdom: What we do for the least, we do for Christ himself. The suffering we encounter in our neighbor is the suffering Christ absorbs in his own heart. When we act with mercy toward another, we both console Jesus and participate in his mission of healing the world.

Daily Devotion (Days 21–23)

For this set of three days, choose one corporal work of mercy and one spiritual work of mercy to practice deliberately. This can be the same corporal and the same spiritual work for all of these three days or distinct works for each day. The key is to actively mark these days with mercy, offered to Jesus through acts for others. Let these not be grand gestures but simple, concrete acts.

Corporal Works of Mercy:

Feed the hungry
Give drink to the thirsty
Clothe the naked
Shelter the homeless
Visit the sick
Visit the imprisoned
Bury the dead

Spiritual Works of Mercy:

Instruct the ignorant
Counsel the doubtful
Admonish sinners
Bear wrongs patiently
Forgive offenses willingly
Comfort the afflicted
Pray for the living and the dead

As you perform these works, do so consciously as an act of devotion to the Sacred Heart. Before acting, pause to remember that this is how Christ's heart beats — moving toward suffering with love. After acting, offer your work to him and pray, "Jesus, I trust in you."

Daily Prayer (Days 21–23)

O Jesus,
You did not remain distant from our suffering
but entered into it completely.
You fed the hungry, healed the sick, and consoled the sorrowful
as you gave your whole life for us.
Form my heart after yours,
that I may love as you love —
not merely with words but with deeds.
Give me eyes to see where mercy is needed,
hands to offer it,
and a heart courageous enough
to enter into suffering with others.
May every work of mercy I perform
allow love to flow from your heart through mine,
consoling you and bringing your warmth to a cold world.
Amen.

DAY 22 | **SAINT**

Faustina Kowalska

O Blood and Water, which gushed forth from the Heart of Jesus as a fount of mercy for us, I trust in you.
–DIARY, 84

Saint John Paul II proclaimed the great Polish nun and mystic as "the great apostle of Divine Mercy in our time." St. Faustina Kowalska was deeply devoted to the Sacred Heart of Jesus, through which and from which all mercy flows. She understood what we have been learning through these days of devotion: The Sacred Heart is not merely an object of contemplation but a living source of mercy that must flow through us to a world grown cold.

When the Lord revealed himself to Saint Faustina, he showed her his pierced Heart as the wellspring of Divine Mercy. The devotion to Divine Mercy that emerged from these revelations and her subsequent diary is strongly tied to the devotion to the Sacred Heart. The blazing love that Margaret Mary beheld in the furnace of Christ's heart, Faustina saw flowing forth as rivers of mercy.

The contrary images of fire and water indicate the unfathomability of the mystery of Jesus' heart: This mystery exceeds even the boundaries of opposing elements. It is also a sign of the wonder of opposing elements meeting in this Sacred Heart, in which Jesus absorbs ingratitude and returns compassion.

This is the heart from which blood and water gushed on Calvary — the fount of mercy for poor sinners, the very same sinners who spurn the Lord.

For Saint Faustina, mercy was not an abstract attribute of God but the very action of divine love moving toward human sin and suffering. She beheld Christ's heart and understood that mercy is love that acts. When love encounters suffering, it does not turn away; it bends down, it enters in, it heals. This is what she saw radiating from the Sacred Heart, not passive pity but active, redemptive love that pursues us in our misery and raises us out of our sin.

In her poetic prayer, Saint Faustina captured the movement from beholding this love to being transformed by it:

> O Eternal Love,
> You command Your Sacred Image to be painted
> And reveal to us the inconceivable fount of mercy,
> You bless whoever approaches Your rays,
> And a soul all black will turn into snow.
> O sweet Jesus, it is here You established the throne of Your mercy
> To bring joy and hope to sinful man.
> From Your open Heart, as from a pure fount,
> Flows comfort to a repentant heart and soul.
> May praise and glory for this Image
> Never cease to stream from man's soul.
> May praise of God's mercy pour from every heart
> Now, and at every hour, and forever and ever.
> (*Diary*, no. 1)[13]

Saint Faustina teaches us that to behold the Sacred Heart is to behold mercy itself. The rays that stream from Christ's Heart — red for blood, pale for water — are the same flames of divine charity that Margaret Mary felt burning within her. But Faustina helps us see even more. These flames are mercy in action; they do not simply warm, they transform. They do not merely console, they heal. A soul "all black" turns to snow under the rays of this merciful heart.

The image of Divine Mercy — Jesus with rays streaming from his pierced heart, bearing the inscription "Jesus, I trust in You" — is another way of presenting the Sacred Heart to the world. It is the same heart, the same love, the same urgent desire to save souls from perdition. Both images call us to behold, to trust, and to become instruments of the mercy we receive.

The Lord told Saint Faustina that mercy must flow through our hearts to others, particularly through works of mercy. As she recorded in her diary, Jesus instructed Faustina: "I demand from you deeds of mercy, which are to arise out of love for Me. You are to show mercy to your neighbors always and everywhere. You must not shrink from this or try to excuse or absolve yourself from it" (*Diary*, no. 742).[14]

The heart that beats within us with a spark of divine charity must beat outward in mercy, or it has not truly learned the rhythm of Christ's own heart. Deeds of mercy are that rhythm. We become like the one we love by the practice of loving others as he has loved us.

Daily Devotion (Days 21–23)

Practice one corporal and one spiritual work of mercy for each of these three days. See day 21 for further instruction.

Daily Prayer (Days 21–23)

O Jesus,
You did not remain distant from our suffering
but entered into it completely.
You fed the hungry, healed the sick, and consoled the sorrowful
as you gave your whole life for us.
Form my heart after yours,
that I may love as you love —
not merely with words but with deeds.
Give me eyes to see where mercy is needed,
hands to offer it,
and a heart courageous enough
to enter into suffering with others.
May every work of mercy I perform
allow love to flow from your heart through mine,
consoling you and bringing your warmth to a cold world.
Amen.

DAY 23 | **THEOLOGY**

On Beholding

Behold this Heart which has so loved men.
–Jesus to St. Margaret Mary Alacoque

To behold is more than to see. When the Lord charges us to "behold" his Sacred Heart, he is not merely directing our eyes but inviting our entire being into an encounter. To behold means to look upon something with sustained attention, with reverence, with an openness to being changed by what we see. The theology of the Sacred Heart is, at its core, a theology of beholding — a contemplation of what happens when human beings truly look upon the love of God made visible in the pierced heart of Jesus.

The devotion to the Sacred Heart of Jesus has always been and always will be proper to the Church's faith, yet this devotion was proposed and propagated in a particular time and in response to particular maladies. In 1928, Pope Pius XI explained one of the specific reasons why, in the wisdom of divine providence, the Sacred Heart was revealed and offered for universal veneration in the Church:

> When the Jansenist heresy, the most crafty of them all, hostile to love and piety towards God, was creeping in and preaching that God was not to be loved as a father but rather to be feared as an implacable judge; then the most benign Jesus showed his own most Sacred Heart to

> the nations lifted up as a standard of peace and charity portending no doubtful victory in the combat.[15]

The Jansenists taught that only a predestined number would be saved, and that outside that number there was no hope of salvation. Relatedly, they held to a rigid interpretation of Saint Augustine's teaching on grace, arguing that human freedom played no part in redemption. Against this coldness, against this terror of divine judgment, Jesus offered his heart for the world to behold. In giving his Sacred Heart, Jesus presented the central disposition of his life, death, and Resurrection: to make manifest the love of God for the life of the world. This love is what directs his heart, and as such it becomes the heart of the world.

What we behold shapes us. The Jansenists beheld an implacable judge and so became fearful, rigid, and despairing. But those who behold the Sacred Heart — like Margaret Mary, John the beloved disciple, Faustina, and us — discover a Father's love, a mercy that pursues, a warmth that melts frozen hearts. To behold the Sacred Heart is to see that we are loved first, loved freely, loved unto death. It is to discover that divine love is not a distant ideal but a beating heart that suffers with us and for us.

To "behold" is both a gift and a mission. It is a gift because the Lord shows us his heart freely, without our deserving it. It is mission because what we behold we must make visible to others. Saint Faustina offered the image of Divine Mercy. Margaret Mary promoted devotion to the Sacred Heart. John took Mary into his home. So we, having beheld the Heart of Christ, must live in such a way that others can behold through us the love we have received.

Daily Devotion (Days 21–23)

Practice one corporal and one spiritual work of mercy for each of these three days. See day 21 for further instruction.

Daily Prayer (Days 21–23)

O Jesus,
You did not remain distant from our suffering
but entered into it completely.
You fed the hungry, healed the sick, and consoled the sorrowful
as you gave your whole life for us.
Form my heart after yours,
that I may love as you love —
not merely with words but with deeds.
Give me eyes to see where mercy is needed,
hands to offer it,
and a heart courageous enough
to enter into suffering with others.
May every work of mercy I perform
allow love to flow from your heart through mine,
consoling you and bringing your warmth to a cold world.
Amen.

Part 7
Hope

DAY 24 | **DEVOTION**

Novena to the Sacred Heart

Ask, and it will be given you; seek, and you will find; knock, and it will be opened to you.

–MATTHEW 7:7

To pray a novena is to learn the rhythm of persistence in hope. The practice of praying for nine consecutive days teaches us what it means to abide in prayer, to return again and again with the same petition, the same openness, the same trust. A novena is not a formula for manipulating God's will but a school of desire. Here we learn to want what God wants to give and to ask with the confidence of children who know their Father's generosity.

The Novena to the Sacred Heart of Jesus emerged as a natural flowering from the revelations to Saint Margaret Mary. Having been drawn into the burning furnace of Christ's love, having beheld the wounds that shine like suns, the Church began to knock persistently at the door of the Sacred Heart, asking for the graces that flow so abundantly from this divine source. This novena holds a particular place in the treasury of devotions to the Sacred Heart, connecting us to the ancient practice of the apostles, who spent nine days in prayer between the Ascension and Pentecost.

What are we doing when we pray this novena? We are doing what Jesus himself invited us to do: We knock, we seek, we ask. But we do not knock at any door; we knock at the very heart of mercy itself. We do not seek just anywhere; we seek in the place where divine love has been poured out without measure. When we pray this novena, we stand in the company of the beloved disciple and all the saints who have learned to rest upon the breast of the Savior and to trust in the promises that beat within his heart.

The Sacred Heart Novena is most traditionally prayed during the nine days leading up to the solemnity of the Sacred Heart of Jesus, which falls on the Friday nineteen days after Pentecost. The heart of Jesus is revealed after the gift of the Spirit is received, for it is the Spirit who opens our eyes to behold the love of the Father in the Son. But the novena also prepares our hearts for the memorial of the Immaculate Heart of Mary, celebrated the day after the solemnity of the Sacred Heart. Mary's heart leads us to her Son's heart, and his heart is most perfectly known through hers. When we pray this novena, we do so with Mary, through Mary, in imitation of Mary.

The saints who loved the Sacred Heart most deeply often made this novena not just once a year but a daily practice. They understood that persistence in prayer is not about changing God's mind but about changing our own hearts. Each day we pray this novena, we knock again at the door of mercy. This repetition is not vain; it is formative. Like water wearing away stone, the gentle persistence of daily prayer gradually reshapes our hearts after the pattern of Christ's own.

We might consider praying this novena over these three days as a mini-novena of initial formation. In it we join ourselves to all those saints and disciples who have learned to trust completely in the promises of the Sacred Heart. We bring our particular intentions and place them within that burning furnace of love. Our part is simply to knock, to seek, to ask — and then to trust. "Sacred Heart of Jesus, I place all my trust in you."

Daily Prayer (Days 24–26)

(Begin each day by identifying a particular intention.)

O my Jesus, you have said:
"Truly I say to you,
ask and it will be given you,
seek and you will find,
knock and it will be opened to you."
Behold I knock, I seek, and ask for the grace of [insert your intention].
Our Father …
Hail Mary …
Glory be to the Father …

Sacred Heart of Jesus, I place all my trust in you.

O my Jesus, you have said:
"Truly I say to you,
if you ask any thing of the Father in my name,
He will give it to you."
Behold, in your name, I ask the Father for the grace of [insert your intention].
Our Father …
Hail Mary …
Glory be to the Father …

Sacred Heart of Jesus, I place all my trust in you.

O my Jesus, you have said:
"Truly I say to you,
heaven and earth will pass away

but my words will not pass away."
Encouraged by your infallible words, I now ask for the grace of [insert your intention].
Our Father …
Hail Mary …
Glory be to the Father …

Sacred Heart of Jesus, I place all my trust in you.

O Sacred Heart of Jesus, for whom it is impossible not to have compassion on the afflicted, have pity on us miserable sinners and grant us the grace which we ask of you, through the Sorrowful and Immaculate Heart of Mary, your tender mother and ours.

Hail, Holy Queen, Mother of Mercy,
our life, our sweetness, and our hope.
To thee do we cry,
poor banished children of Eve.
To thee do we send up our sighs,
mourning and weeping in this valley of tears.
Turn then, most gracious advocate,
thine eyes of mercy toward us,
and after this our exile
show unto us the blessed fruit of thy womb, Jesus.
O clement, O loving,
O sweet Virgin Mary.
Amen.

Saint Joseph, foster father of Jesus, pray for us.

DAY 25 | **SAINT**

Padre Pio of Pietrelcina

Pray, hope, and don't worry.
God is merciful and will hear your prayer.
—POPULARLY ATTRIBUTED TO PADRE PIO

In the twentieth century, a humble Capuchin friar in southern Italy became one of the Sacred Heart's most fervent apostles. St. Pio of Pietrelcina — known to the world as Padre Pio — lived this mystery not only in prayer but in his very flesh. For fifty years, from 1918 until his death in 1968, he bore the visible wounds of Christ's passion: the stigmata. His hands, feet, and side bled continuously, drawing countless souls to behold the suffering love of the Savior made visible.

But before the world could see his wounds, Padre Pio had already been pierced invisibly in his heart. On August 5, 1918, while hearing confessions, he experienced the *transverberation* — a mystical piercing of the heart by divine love. He described it: "While I was confessing some friars, I was overcome by such immense pain that it felt as though my heart had been pierced by a lance of fire."[16] This invisible wound preceded the visible stigmata by six weeks. Like Margaret Mary before him, Padre Pio learned that to love the Sacred Heart means sharing not only in his ardent charity but also in his redemptive suffering.

Padre Pio understood what John the beloved disciple and Margaret Mary had discovered: that love and suffering cannot be separated in the Sacred Heart of Jesus. The Lord who burns with love for sinners is the same Lord who endures the coldness of human ingratitude. To rest upon the breast of the Savior, as Padre Pio did daily in his celebration of Mass and in his hours before the Blessed Sacrament, is to feel both the warmth of divine charity and the wounds inflicted by our rejection of that love.

Every day Padre Pio prayed the novena to the Sacred Heart that we are praying during these three days. This prayer became his instrument of intercession. Countless people asked Padre Pio for his prayers. He responded by taking their intentions into the furnace of the Sacred Heart through this novena. Day after day, he knocked at the door of divine mercy, confident in the promises that would not pass away. Many who asked experienced miraculous healings and conversions through the power of the Sacred Heart to which he brought every petition.

Padre Pio's famous counsel, "Pray, hope, and don't worry," came not from easy optimism but from a life soaked in suffering and prayer. He spent countless hours in the confessional, often from before dawn until late at night, hearing the sins and sorrows of thousands of souls. He celebrated Mass with such intensity that witnesses said watching him was to watch a man utterly consumed by love. Through it all, the wounds in his hands bled, the pain in his side persisted, and yet he continued to pray the novena to the Sacred Heart, day after day, for a world in need of mercy.

In his devotion to the Sacred Heart, Padre Pio manifested what one spiritual writer described as "mystical union, in a faithful imitation, a loving reparation and confident prayer."[17] He was united to Christ's heart through the wounds they shared. He imitated Christ's heart through his tireless service to souls. He offered reparation to Christ's heart for the ingratitude that wounded it. And he prayed with confidence to Christ's heart, trusting in the promises Jesus had made.

As we continue praying the novena these days, we pray in the company of Padre Pio. We join our petitions to his, our trust to his, and our hope to his. We knock, seek, and ask as he did. And we trust, as he trusted, that the heart that could not refuse his prayers will not refuse ours.

Daily Prayer (Days 24–26)

(Begin each day by identifying a particular intention.)
O my Jesus, you have said:
"Truly I say to you,
ask and it will be given you,
seek and you will find,
knock and it will be opened to you."
Behold I knock, I seek and ask for the grace of [insert your intention].
Our Father …
Hail Mary …
Glory be to the Father …

Sacred Heart of Jesus, I place all my trust in you.

O my Jesus, you have said:
"Truly I say to you,
if you ask any thing of the Father in my name,
He will give it to you."
Behold, in your name, I ask the Father for the grace of [insert your intention].
Our Father …
Hail Mary …
Glory be to the Father …

Sacred Heart of Jesus, I place all my trust in you.

O my Jesus, you have said:
"Truly I say to you,
heaven and earth will pass away
but my words will not pass away."
Encouraged by your infallible words, I now ask for the
grace of [insert your intention].
Our Father …
Hail Mary …
Glory be to the Father …

Sacred Heart of Jesus, I place all my trust in you.

O Sacred Heart of Jesus, for whom it is impossible not to have compassion on the afflicted, have pity on us miserable sinners and grant us the grace which we ask of you, through the Sorrowful and Immaculate Heart of Mary, your tender mother and ours.

Hail, Holy Queen, Mother of Mercy,
our life, our sweetness, and our hope.
To thee do we cry,
poor banished children of Eve.
To thee do we send up our sighs,
mourning and weeping in this valley of tears.
Turn then, most gracious advocate,
thine eyes of mercy toward us,
and after this our exile
show unto us the blessed fruit of thy womb, Jesus.
O clement, O loving,
O sweet Virgin Mary.
Amen.

Saint Joseph, foster father of Jesus, pray for us.

DAY 26 | **THEOLOGY**

The Decision

He asked for my heart, which I asked him to take,
which he did and then placed myself
in his own adorable heart.
–St. Margaret Mary Alacoque[18]

For three days we are praying the novena to the Sacred Heart, knocking at the door of divine mercy as Padre Pio did daily. We bring our petitions and the needs of others before this heart, trusting in Christ's promises. This act of prayer is not merely a request for favors; it is a decision — a choice to respond to what the Sacred Heart offers. The Sacred Heart is revealed as both gift and proposal. It is a gift in that we are invited to adore the heart by which divine love was poured out for the world. It is a proposal in that this heart invites our acceptance, our love, our response. Between the gift and our reception of it stands the decision.

To behold the Sacred Heart is not merely to turn back the clock and adore Jesus only as he was in Gethsemane and Golgotha when he bore the ingratitude and sinfulness of the world. Rather, beholding that heart means encountering him in his hard-wrought love now; we encounter the One who, having suffered, is now risen. He has entered into his glory, but only as the one who suffered, died, and was buried. The Risen One is the Crucified One. Contemplating and drawing near to his suffering is the path to beholding him in glory.

Our response to the Sacred Heart matters. When we pray the novena for others, as Padre Pio did, we are not merely asking for favors — we are offering reparation. Pope Pius XI taught that love must be given in return for love, and when that love has been neglected or violated, "some sort of compensation must be rendered for the injury, and this debt is commonly called by the name of reparation."[19] It matters that some part of humanity receives and responds to the love of God in Christ, that some sinners on behalf of the many willfully accept Christ's sacrificial offering. When we pray for others, when we offer our prayers and sufferings in union with the Sacred Heart, we become instruments of consolation to the Lord.

This is what Padre Pio understood when he prayed the novena daily for all who asked his intercession. He was offering himself in union with Christ's suffering for the salvation of souls. Those who undertake this devotion — accepting and offering themselves to the suffering love of the Savior — become sharers in the reconciliation of the one Body of Christ. Saint Augustine expressed this mystery: "Christ suffered whatever it behooved him to suffer; now nothing is wanting of the measure of the sufferings. Therefore, the sufferings were fulfilled, but in the head; there were yet remaining the sufferings of Christ in his body."[20] Christ's sufferings are not repeated. When his disciples offer themselves in union with his sufferings — undergone once for all — the members of Christ's Body are being united to Christ the Head in what he alone suffered. Being united to him in suffering is the means for being united to him in glory.

The theology of the Sacred Heart is a theology of grace and freedom. It is about the incarnate love of God poured out in Christ and it is about our freedom to respond. The choice to pray the novena, to offer ourselves for others, to rest upon the Savior's breast and remain with him in suffering — these are the decisions by which we enter into communion with Christ. In praying as Padre Pio prayed and responding as the saints responded, we make our decision: to accept the gift, to answer the proposal, to give our hearts to the Sacred Heart. In the end, there is only one Christ — him in us and us in him.

Daily Prayer (Days 24–26)

(Begin each day by identifying a particular intention.)
O my Jesus, you have said:
"Truly I say to you,
ask and it will be given you,
seek and you will find,
knock and it will be opened to you."
Behold I knock, I seek and ask for the grace of [insert your intention].
Our Father …
Hail Mary …
Glory be to the Father …

Sacred Heart of Jesus, I place all my trust in you.

O my Jesus, you have said:
"Truly I say to you,
if you ask any thing of the Father in my name,
He will give it to you."
Behold, in your name, I ask the Father for the grace of [insert your intention].
Our Father …
Hail Mary …
Glory be to the Father …

Sacred Heart of Jesus, I place all my trust in you.

O my Jesus, you have said:
"Truly I say to you,
heaven and earth will pass away
but my words will not pass away."
Encouraged by your infallible words, I now ask for the grace of [insert your intention].
Our Father …
Hail Mary …
Glory be to the Father …

Sacred Heart of Jesus, I place all my trust in you.

O Sacred Heart of Jesus, for whom it is impossible not to have compassion on the afflicted, have pity on us miserable sinners and grant us the grace which we ask of you, through the Sorrowful and Immaculate Heart of Mary, your tender mother and ours.

Hail, Holy Queen, Mother of Mercy,
our life, our sweetness, and our hope.
To thee do we cry,
poor banished children of Eve.
To thee do we send up our sighs,
mourning and weeping in this valley of tears.
Turn then, most gracious advocate,
thine eyes of mercy toward us,
and after this our exile
show unto us the blessed fruit of thy womb, Jesus.
O clement, O loving,
O sweet Virgin Mary.
Amen.

Saint Joseph, foster father of Jesus, pray for us.

INTERLUDE 3 | **THE LITANY OF THE SACRED HEART**

A litany is an ancient form of prayer by repetition — invocation after invocation, each one building upon the last, each one forming us more deeply into the mystery we approach. The litany does not explain; it invites. It does not argue; it adores. Through repetition, the invocations become a rhythm that shapes our hearts to the cadence of divine love. For the next three days, we will pray and contemplate the Litany of the Sacred Heart of Jesus.

The Church has always known that repetition is the language of the heart. A child learns how to express love from hearing "I love you" spoken again and again. A disciple learns devotion by returning daily to the same words that carry us to God. In the litany we discover that faithful repetition is formative. Each invocation — "Heart of Jesus, Son of the eternal Father," "Heart of Jesus, holy temple of God," "Heart of Jesus, source of all consolation" — washes over us like waves, each one leaving its mark, each one drawing us deeper into the ocean of Christ's love.

Over these next three days, we will contemplate the litany in three movements:

1. First, according to that which we can only praise
2. Second, according to that which we ask for in our need
3. Third, according to how union with this heart changes who we become

These three movements trace the arc of all Christian life: adoration, petition, and transformation. They are the rhythm of the Sacred Heart itself, which burns with the glory of the Father, bends low to bear our sins, and raises us to new life in the Spirit.

As you pray the Litany of the Sacred Heart over these days, do not rush. Let each invocation rest in you. Feel the rhythm build. Allow your heart to beat to this rhythmic prayer, until prayer and pulse become one.

Part 8

The Litany

LITANY OF THE SACRED HEART OF JESUS

Lord, have mercy. Lord, have mercy.
Christ, have mercy. Christ, have mercy.
Lord, have mercy. Lord, have mercy.
God our Father in heaven, have mercy on us.
God the Son, Redeemer of the world, have mercy on us.
God the Holy Spirit, have mercy on us.
Holy Trinity, one God, have mercy on us.

Holy Mary, pray for us.

Heart of Jesus, Son of the eternal Father, have mercy on us.
Heart of Jesus, formed by the Holy Spirit in the womb of the Virgin Mother, have mercy on us.
Heart of Jesus, one with the eternal Word, have mercy on us.
Heart of Jesus, infinite in majesty, have mercy on us.
Heart of Jesus, holy temple of God, have mercy on us.
Heart of Jesus, tabernacle of the Most High, have mercy on us.
Heart of Jesus, house of God and gate of heaven, have mercy on us.
Heart of Jesus, aflame with love for us, have mercy on us.
Heart of Jesus, source of justice and love, have mercy on us.
Heart of Jesus, full of goodness and love, have mercy on us.
Heart of Jesus, wellspring of all virtue, have mercy on us.
Heart of Jesus, worthy of all praise, have mercy on us.
Heart of Jesus, king and center of all hearts, have mercy

on us.

Heart of Jesus, treasure-house of wisdom and knowledge, have mercy on us.

Heart of Jesus, in whom there dwells the fullness of God, have mercy on us.

Heart of Jesus, in whom the Father is well pleased, have mercy on us.

Heart of Jesus, from whose fullness we have all received, have mercy on us.

Heart of Jesus, desire of the eternal hills, have mercy on us.

Heart of Jesus, patient and full of mercy, have mercy on us.

Heart of Jesus, generous to all who turn to you, have mercy on us.

Heart of Jesus, fountain of life and holiness, have mercy on us.

Heart of Jesus, atonement for our sins, have mercy on us.

Heart of Jesus, overwhelmed with insults, have mercy on us.

Heart of Jesus, broken for our sins, have mercy on us.

Heart of Jesus, obedient even to death, have mercy on us.

Heart of Jesus, pierced by a lance, have mercy on us.

Heart of Jesus, source of all consolation, have mercy on us.

Heart of Jesus, our life and resurrection, have mercy on us.

Heart of Jesus, our peace and reconciliation, have mercy on us.

Heart of Jesus, victim of our sins, have mercy on us.

Heart of Jesus, salvation of all who trust in you, have mercy on us.

Heart of Jesus, hope of all who die in you, have mercy on

us.
Heart of Jesus, delight of all the saints, have mercy on us.

Lamb of God, you take away the sins of the world, have mercy on us.
Lamb of God, you take away the sins of the world, have mercy on us.
Lamb of God, you take away the sins of the world, have mercy on us.

Jesus, gentle and humble of heart.

Touch our hearts and make them like your own.

Let us pray.

Grant, we pray, almighty God, that we, who glory in the heart of your beloved Son and recall the wonders of his love for us, may be made worthy to receive an overflowing measure of grace from that fount of heavenly gifts. Through Christ our Lord.

Amen.

DAY 27 | **LITANY OF THE SACRED HEART**

The Heart That We Adore

Heart of Jesus, infinite in majesty. ...
Heart of Jesus, worthy of all praise. ...
Heart of Jesus, king and center of all hearts.
–FROM THE LITANY OF THE SACRED HEART

The Litany of the Sacred Heart begins with praise. Before we bring our needs, before we name our sins, we simply behold. We gaze upon the heart of Jesus and name what is true. This heart is infinite in majesty, the holy temple of God, a treasure-house of wisdom and knowledge. These invocations declare what is: This is the heart that dwells in the fullness of God, the heart in which the Father is well pleased, the heart that is king and center of all hearts.

To praise is to see rightly. When we praise the Sacred Heart, we train our eyes to see what is already there. We learn to perceive reality as it truly is. The Sacred Heart of Jesus is infinite in majesty because God the Son has taken on human flesh and a human heart that beats with divine love. This heart is the holy temple of God — the dwelling place where heaven and earth meet. This heart is worthy of all praise because we need to speak these words, to align ourselves with the truth of who Jesus is.

When we follow the litany in naming the heart of Jesus as "one with the eternal Word," "formed by the Holy Spirit in the womb of the Virgin Mother," and "Son of the eternal Father," we stand on holy ground. These are revelations God has given us. The litany places these mysteries on our lips and in our hearts so that we might enter into them more deeply. Each time we pray, "Heart of Jesus, house of God and gate of heaven," we position ourselves before the threshold of divine love. We learn where to stand.

Praising the Sacred Heart forms us. It shapes our desires. When we repeatedly name this heart as "aflame with love for us. … source of justice and love. … full of goodness and love," we train our hearts to long for what is true, good, and beautiful. We are formed to desire what God knows we need: union with this heart that burns for us.

To praise the Sacred Heart is to consent to be changed by it. When we name this heart as "wellspring of all virtue" and "fountain of life and holiness," we open ourselves to receive from this wellspring, to drink from this fountain. We say: Let this heart be for me what it truly is — source, center, treasure, king.

Saint Irenaeus taught that "the glory of God is a human being fully alive."[21] When we praise the Sacred Heart, we come alive to the glory of God dwelling among us. We wake up to the reality that has always been true: The heart of Jesus is infinite in majesty, and that heart beats for us. Our praise makes us true — true to ourselves, true to our deepest longing, true to the God who made us for himself.

As you pray the Litany of the Sacred Heart today, linger over the invocations of praise. Let these words of adoration rest in you. Let them form your heart to the rhythm of divine love. Let them teach you to see the Sacred Heart as it truly is — infinite, holy, glorious — and beating for you.

Prayer

Heart of Jesus, worthy of all praise:
I offer you my adoration.
Open my eyes to see you as you are.
Train my heart to desire you above all things.
Let my prayer become my pulse,
    beating in time with your own.
Form me by the rhythm of your love,
    until I am fully alive to your glory.
Amen.

Today's Mantra

Heart of Jesus, worthy of all praise, have mercy on me.

DAY 28 | **LITANY OF THE SACRED HEART**

The Heart That Bears Our Sins

Heart of Jesus, broken for our sins. ...
Heart of Jesus, overwhelmed with insults. ...
Heart of Jesus, obedient even to death.
–FROM THE LITANY OF THE SACRED HEART

After we have praised God, we bring him our need. The Litany of the Sacred Heart does not remain in the realm of glory. It descends with Jesus into the depths of human suffering and sin. The invocations shift: from infinite majesty to "atonement for our sins," from holy temple to "overwhelmed with insults," from king of all hearts to "broken for our sins." But the heart that is infinite in majesty and the heart that is pierced by a lance are one and the same. The glory and the suffering are united.

These invocations name what Jesus endured for our sake. "Heart of Jesus, overwhelmed with insults" — here we name the mockery, the spitting, the crown of thorns. "Heart of Jesus, broken for our sins" — here we acknowledge that what broke this heart was the weight of human ingratitude, betrayal, and rejection. "Heart of Jesus, obedient even to death" — here we bow before the mystery that divine love chose the path of suffering because love always bears the cost of redemption.

When we pray these invocations, we face the present reality of sin and acknowledge that sin has wounded the heart of Jesus. Again, as Pope Pius XI taught, if love "has been neglected by forgetfulness or violated by offense, some sort of compensation must be rendered for the injury, and this debt is commonly called by the name of reparation."[22] The litany brings us face-to-face with this need. We cannot undo the past, but we can offer the heart of Jesus our sorrow, our repentance, our desire to console where we have caused pain.

When we pray, "Heart of Jesus, atonement for our sins," we name both our guilt and God's mercy. This heart is our atonement. This is the heart that bears what we cannot bear, that accomplishes what we cannot accomplish.

To pray "Heart of Jesus, victim of our sins" is to stand in the place of truth. Our sins — my envy, my pride, my coldness of heart — these are what pierced his heart. Yet the litany does not leave us in despair. It immediately follows with "salvation of all who trust in you." The heart that we wounded is the heart that saves us. The wounds we inflicted have become the wellspring of our healing.

Saint Augustine wrote, "Christ suffered whatever it behooved him to suffer; now nothing is wanting of the measure of the sufferings. Therefore, the sufferings were fulfilled, but in the head; there were yet remaining the sufferings of Christ in his body."[23] Christ's suffering was complete, once for all. The litany invites us to enter into that suffering, to unite ourselves to it. When we pray these invocations, we accept our share in the mystery of redemption.

Love draws near to the beloved's suffering. When we pray, "Heart of Jesus, overwhelmed with insults," and "Heart of Jesus, pierced by a lance," we learn to remain with Jesus in his suffering, as Mary and John did at the foot of the cross. We ask for the grace to feel in our own hearts some small portion of what he felt in his.

Our prayer matters. Our sorrow matters. Our desire to console the heart of Jesus matters. We can offer love in return for love, devotion in return for sacrifice, faithfulness in return for the fidelity that endured the cross. The litany gives us the words to make this offering, invocation by invocation, until our hearts are formed to both the sorrow and the mercy of the Sacred Heart.

As you pray the litany today kneel, before the invocations of Christ's suffering. Let them pierce your heart as the lance pierced his. Offer your heart to the heart that was broken for you, and trust that in this exchange, both hearts — his and yours — beat as one.

Prayer

Heart of Jesus, broken for our sins:
I offer you my sorrow.
I cannot undo what has been done,
    but I can offer you my love in return for yours.
Teach me to remain with you in your suffering.
Let my repentance be true,
    my love be sincere,
    and my devotion be faithful.
Make my heart a source of consolation to you,
    even as yours is the source of my salvation.
Amen.

Today's Mantra

Heart of Jesus, pierced for my sins, have mercy on me.

DAY 29 | **LITANY OF THE SACRED HEART**

The Heart That Makes Us New

Heart of Jesus, source of all consolation. …
Heart of Jesus, our life and resurrection. …
Heart of Jesus, our peace and reconciliation.
—FROM THE LITANY OF THE SACRED HEART

The litany does not end in sorrow. After we have praised the glory of the Sacred Heart and entered into the mystery of its suffering, the invocations turn toward what this heart accomplishes in us. The final movement names transformation: "Heart of Jesus, source of all consolation"; "Heart of Jesus, our life and resurrection"; "Heart of Jesus, our peace and reconciliation." These invocations reveal that the Sacred Heart changes who we become.

When we pray, "Heart of Jesus, source of all consolation," we ask to become sources of consolation for others. The Sacred Heart pours out its gifts through us. If this heart is the source of all consolation, then we who draw near to this heart become channels of that consolation. We become instruments of the mercy we have received.

This is the great mystery of the Christian life: What we receive from Christ we give to others. What Christ is for us, we become for the world. Saint Paul wrote, "Blessed be … the God of all comfort, who comforts us in all our affliction, so that we may be able to comfort those who are in any affliction, with the comfort with which we ourselves are comforted by God" (2 Cor 1:3–4). The litany of the Sacred Heart forms us into this reality. We pray to become like the heart of Jesus.

"Heart of Jesus, our life and resurrection" — this invocation speaks of life now, in the midst of death. It speaks of the power of the Resurrection at work in our mortal bodies, in our failing relationships, in our broken communities. The heart of Jesus refuses to let death have the final word. When we unite ourselves to this heart, we participate in its Resurrection life. We become agents of new life in a world addicted to despair.

"Heart of Jesus, our peace and reconciliation" — here the litany names what the world most desperately needs. The Sacred Heart is the place where all things are gathered up, where heaven and earth embrace, where God and humanity are united. When we pray this invocation, we ask to receive peace and to become peacemakers, to receive reconciliation and to become ministers of reconciliation.

The transformation the litany speaks of is configuration to Christ. It is the work of the Spirit, who conforms us to Christ from the inside out. As we pray these invocations day after day — "Heart of Jesus, fountain of life and holiness"; "Heart of Jesus, salvation of all who trust in you"; "Heart of Jesus, hope of all who die in you" — the words reshape us, wearing away our resistance, reforming our desires, forming us into living images of the heart we invoke.

St. Margaret Mary Alacoque once wrote, "He asked for my heart, which I asked him to take, which he did and then placed myself in his own adorable heart."[24] This is what the litany accomplishes over time: an exchange of hearts. We offer our small, fearful hearts to Jesus, and he places them in his own Sacred Heart, where they are purified, expanded, set aflame. Then he returns our hearts to us, transformed. They are still ours, but now they beat with his rhythm; now they burn with his love.

The final invocations point us toward heaven: "Heart of Jesus, hope of all who die in you"; "Heart of Jesus, delight of all the saints." Our transformation is not yet complete. We are being formed, day by day, into the people we will one day be in God's presence. The saints already dwell in the Sacred Heart fully. We are on the way, being drawn ever closer by the invocations we pray, the devotions we practice, the love we allow to reshape us.

As you pray the litany today, pay attention to the invocations of transformation. Let them speak to you of what you are becoming: a source of consolation, a bearer of life, an agent of peace. These changes are occurring not by your own power but by union with the Sacred Heart: day by day, invocation by invocation, heartbeat by heartbeat.

Prayer

Heart of Jesus, our life and resurrection:
I offer you my yes.
Transform me into your image.
Make me a source of consolation to those who suffer,
a bearer of life to those who despair,
an agent of peace in a world of division.
Let my heart beat in time with yours
until I am fully conformed to your love.
Make me for others what you are for me:
gift, mercy, life.
Amen.

Today's Mantra

Heart of Jesus, make my heart like yours.

INTERLUDE 4 | **THE PROMISES OF THE SACRED HEART**

We have journeyed through twenty-nine days of devotion to the Sacred Heart of Jesus. We have drawn near, remained, and responded. We have contemplated the revelations to Saint Margaret Mary, we have prayed the novena, and we have meditated on the litany. Through all of this we have been formed — slowly, steadily — with a heart renewed in Jesus.

The devotion to the Sacred Heart produces, in the end, one ultimate, marvelous fruit: a heart like Jesus' own. Near the end of the Litany of the Sacred Heart, we pray, "Jesus, gentle and humble of heart, touch our hearts and make them like your own." This is what we have been asking for all along. Gentleness and humility shape the heart of the one who follows Jesus in penitence and adoration. The gift bestowed to those devoted to the Sacred Heart is to become like the one you love. The heart that adores the Sacred Heart becomes what the Sacred Heart is: a dwelling place for divine love.

Jesus revealed to Saint Margaret Mary twelve promises for those who dedicate themselves to his Sacred Heart. These promises are his pledge to make our devotion truly fruitful. To adore his heart is an act of faith, trusting that his promises are true. We cannot taste this fruit beforehand; it is only through the devotion itself that these fruits become available. Jesus asks for trust and dedication, and he rewards those who trust in him with a steady share in his own charity.

Over these final four days, we will contemplate the twelve promises according to four movements of grace: healing, strengthening, sanctifying, and abiding. This progression reaches down to our creaturely weakness — both in sin and in affliction — moves us forward in steps of strengthening, grows toward sanctification, and ultimately arrives at the gift of abiding in union with the Sacred Heart.

Part 9

The Promises

THE TWELVE PROMISES OF THE SACRED HEART

The twelve promises are drawn from a series of Saint Margaret Mary's letters. Each is presented in the voice of Jesus, whom Saint Margaret Mary credits as speaking these promises to her over the course of their encounters and through her sustained reflection on the mysteries of the Sacred Heart.[25]

1. "I will comfort them in all their afflictions."
2. "Sinners shall find in My Heart the source and the infinite ocean of mercy."
3. "I promise you in the excessive mercy of My Heart that My all-powerful love will grant to all those who shall receive communion on the First Friday in nine consecutive months the grace of final penance; they shall not die in My disgrace nor without receiving their sacraments; My Divine Heart shall be their safe refuge in this last moment."
4. "I will give them all of the graces necessary for their state of life."
5. "I will bestow a large blessing upon all their undertakings."
6. "I will give to priests the gift of touching the most hardened hearts."
7. "I will be their strength during life and above all during death."
8. "Tepid souls shall grow fervent."
9. "Fervent souls shall quickly mount to higher perfection."
10. "I will establish peace in their houses."
11. "I will bless every place where a picture of My Heart shall be set up and honored."

12. "Those who shall promote this devotion shall have their names written in My Heart, never to be blotted out."

DAY 30 | THE PROMISES OF THE SACRED HEART

The Gift of Healing

I will comfort them in all their afflictions.
–FIRST PROMISE OF THE SACRED HEART

The first movement of the Sacred Heart toward us is healing. The Lord comes to us in our weakness, in our sin, in our mortality — and he restores what we cannot restore ourselves.

The three promises of healing that Jesus makes to those devoted to his Sacred Heart are these:

1. "I will comfort them in all their afflictions."
2. "Sinners shall find in My Heart the source and the infinite ocean of mercy."
3. "I promise you in the excessive mercy of My Heart that My all-powerful love will grant to all those who shall receive communion on the First Friday in nine consecutive months the grace of final penance; they shall not die in My disgrace nor without receiving their sacraments; My Divine Heart shall be their safe refuge in this last moment."

These promises meet us precisely where we need to be met. Consider the first: comfort in all our afflictions. This is assurance of consolation throughout the trials of life — the perils of finitude, the cost of sacrifices, the weight of sorrow. When we are weak, we discover that we are strong, not by our own power but by union with the Sacred Heart.

The second promise addresses sin directly. Whenever our weakness takes the form of rebellion, ingratitude, or coldness of heart, we find healing in Christ's mercy. We do not approach this heart as the righteous come to the righteous. We come as sinners to an infinite ocean, ready to receive us and make us clean.

The third promise extends to our final hour. Even death — the last enemy — cannot separate us from this love. The Lord Jesus offers his own heart as refuge in our last moment. Those who practice the First Friday devotion can trust that when death comes, the Sacred Heart will be their safety and their home.

Saint Paul wrote, "When I am weak, then I am strong" (2 Cor 12:10). This is the paradox at the heart of these promises. Our weakness is not denied or dismissed. The Sacred Heart meets us in our actual condition and transforms weakness into strength, sin into mercy, death into life.

What the Sacred Heart offers is not merely therapeutic comfort. When Christ heals, he does not simply repair damage or return us to a prior state. He makes us new. The healing we receive prepares us for everything that follows: the strengthening, the sanctifying, and the abiding that are yet to come.

As you pray today, bring your afflictions to the Sacred Heart. Name your sins before this infinite ocean of mercy. Entrust your final hour to this safe refuge. The Lord who was pierced for your sake now heals all that needs healing in you.

Prayer

Sacred Heart of Jesus, source and infinite ocean of mercy:
I bring you all my weakness.
Heal my afflictions,
    wash away my sins,
    and be my refuge in the hour of my death.
I trust in your promise to comfort, to forgive, and to save.
Make me whole by your pierced heart,
    that I may be prepared for all you desire to give me.
Amen.

Today's Mantra

Sacred Heart of Jesus, heal me and make me whole.

DAY 31 | THE PROMISES OF THE SACRED HEART

The Gift of Strengthening

I will give them all of the graces necessary for their state of life.
—FOURTH PROMISE OF THE SACRED HEART

After healing comes strengthening. The Sacred Heart does not only restore health to Christ's friends; it builds them up in strength, making them capable of service in this world. The Lord heals us in order to equip us, to empower us, and to send us forth.

The three promises of strengthening speak to this empowerment:

1. "I will give them all of the graces necessary for their state of life."
2. "I will bestow a large blessing upon all their undertakings."
3. "I will give to priests the gift of touching the most hardened hearts."

The Lord recognizes the diversity of gifts within his one body. Each of us has a particular calling, a specific state of life, a unique mission. The Sacred Heart pledges to equip us with everything we need for our vocation. Whatever God calls us to, he will supply the grace to accomplish it. We need only remain devoted to his heart.

The blessings Christ gives are not meager or cautious. They are large — more than sufficient — for the activities of charity to which we are called. When we undertake works of love, works of mercy, or works of justice, the Sacred Heart blesses these undertakings abundantly. We become filled with divine bounty for the discharge of our duties. Our efforts bear fruit because they are rooted in the Sacred Heart.

The promise to priests is particular and powerful. Those called to the ministerial priesthood and who are devoted to the Sacred Heart will find success in their ministry of preaching and healing. Even those most opposed to the love of God will find, through the power coursing through these priests, the very love they most desperately need. The Sacred Heart works through its priests to reach the unreachable.

These promises of strengthening reveal a fundamental truth: Devotion to the Sacred Heart is not private piety. It is preparation for mission. When we adore the Sacred Heart, we are equipped for service. When we receive from the Sacred Heart, we are empowered to give. The strength that flows from Christ's heart courses through our own hearts, making us capable of strengthening others with the strength of Christ.

We are not spectators of divine love. We become participants, agents, extensions of the Sacred Heart in the world. The strength we receive is strength for service, strength for sacrifice, strength for love.

As you pray today, ask for the graces necessary for your state of life. Bring your undertakings before the Sacred Heart and ask for blessing. Pray for those called to the priesthood, that they may receive the gift to touch the hearts of those who seem unreachable. The Lord who strengthens you will not fail you.

Prayer

Sacred Heart of Jesus, source of all strength:
Give me the graces I need for my vocation.
Bless the works of love I undertake in your name.
Make me an instrument of your power,
    that even the hardest hearts
    may be touched by your love through me.
Strengthen me for service,
    that I may give as generously as I have received.
Amen.

Today's Mantra

Sacred Heart of Jesus, strengthen me for your service.

DAY 32 | THE PROMISES OF THE SACRED HEART

The Gift of Sanctifying

Tepid souls shall grow fervent.
–Eighth promise of the Sacred Heart

The fruits of the Sacred Heart do not end with what we become capable of doing. They move to what we ourselves become. After healing and strengthening comes sanctifying — the transformation of the devotee into the very likeness of Christ.

The three promises of sanctifying speak to this progressive transformation:

1. I will be their strength during life and above all during death.
2. Tepid souls shall grow fervent.
3. Fervent souls shall quickly mount to higher perfection.

Those devoted to the Sacred Heart do not merely dispense strength to others; they become strong themselves. Drinking from the source of charity, they become sources of charity. The Sacred Heart is their strength in every moment of life — and most especially in that final moment when all earthly strength fails. The Sacred Heart carries us through death into life.

The promise of kindled fire speaks to those who come to the

Sacred Heart in lukewarmness. Going through the motions distracted, half-hearted — all of this gives way when we draw near to divine love. The fervor of charity is increased, welling up from the Sacred Heart and filling us with divine life. Tepidity yields to zeal. Indifference yields to passion. The cold heart becomes a burning heart, aflame with the love it adores.

For those already fervent, the Sacred Heart promises even greater transformation. They will ascend quickly to higher perfection — not by their own striving but by the power of divine love drawing them upward. The Sacred Heart becomes the energy for greater and greater conformity to Christ, who is the source and summit of all charity.

These promises reveal the Sacred Heart as the furnace of transformation. We are called to be made holy by union with Christ. The Sacred Heart is the refining fire that burns away what is not love, that purifies what is impure, that perfects what is imperfect.

Saint Margaret Mary taught her sisters to "become like the Sacred Heart, meek and humble."[26] This is sanctification: becoming like the one we adore. It happens through devotion itself. As we draw near to the Sacred Heart, as we remain with the Sacred Heart, as we respond to the Sacred Heart, we are changed. We take on the virtues of the divine Heart — gentleness, humility, mercy, love.

Sanctification is transformation. It is the work of the Spirit conforming us to Christ from the inside out. The tepid become fervent, the fervent ascend to perfection, and all who remain faithful find that the Sacred Heart becomes their strength in life and in death.

As you pray today, ask the Sacred Heart to kindle fire in your tepid heart. If you are already fervent, ask to mount higher. Entrust your entire life — and your death — to the strength of the Sacred Heart. Let the sanctifying work continue.

Prayer

Sacred Heart of Jesus, furnace of divine love:
Burn away all that is not love in me.
Kindle fervor where I am tepid.
Raise me to higher perfection where I am fervent.
Be my strength in life and in death.
Transform me by your fire, that I may become like you —
gentle and humble of heart,
wholly conformed to your love.
Amen.

Today's Mantra

Sacred Heart of Jesus, make me holy as you are holy.

DAY 33 | THE PROMISES OF THE SACRED HEART

The Gift of Abiding

I will establish peace in their houses.
–TENTH PROMISE OF THE SACRED HEART

We arrive at the final movement of grace: abiding. This is the culmination of all that has come before — healing, strengthening, sanctifying. The end of God's act of creation, redemption, and sanctification is for us to rest in the love of God and to become a resting place for that love.

The *Catechism* teaches that "the ultimate end of the whole divine economy is the entry of God's creatures into the perfect unity of the Blessed Trinity. But even now we are called to be a dwelling for the Most Holy Trinity" (CCC 260). From his Sacred Heart Jesus promises nothing less than this ultimate fruit: the gift of abiding with God, in God, by the love of God.

The three final promises speak to this abiding:

1. I will establish peace in their houses.
2. I will bless every place where a picture of My Heart shall be set up and honored.
3. Those who shall promote this devotion shall have their names written in My Heart, never to be blotted out.

The first promise seems almost mundane — peace in our homes, in our daily domestic life. But the love that flows from the Sacred Heart makes even the places where we dwell now into antechambers of heaven. The homes where the Sacred Heart is adored become filled with the peace of Christ, the same peace he gives his friends, the peace that will fill all things in the fullness of time. This is peace not as the world gives but as Christ gives — the deep, abiding peace of dwelling in divine love.

The second promise extends this blessing beyond our homes to every place marked by devotion to the Sacred Heart. Wherever the image of the Sacred Heart is enthroned, that space becomes a realm of the kingdom of the Prince of Peace. These are not magical talismans but sacramental signs — visible reminders of the invisible reality that the Sacred Heart desires to dwell with us and in us. To honor the image is to welcome the reality it represents.

The third promise offers eternal abiding. For those who make a dwelling place for the love of God here, the Lord will keep their names written in his own heart. He will give them an everlasting dwelling place with him who abides in the Father and with whom the Father abides. This is the fulfillment of Jesus' prayer: "that they may all be one, as you, Father, are in me and I in you, that they also may be in us" (Jn 17:21).

The heart that adores the Sacred Heart becomes what the Sacred Heart is: a dwelling place for divine love.

This is where our thirty-three days have been leading. We began by learning to draw near to the Sacred Heart, to place ourselves upon the breast of the Savior as John did. We learned to remain with the Sacred Heart even in suffering, as Mary did. We learned to respond to the commandment to love as we have been loved. We contemplated the revelations, prayed the novena, and meditated on the litany. Through all of this, we have been prepared for abiding.

To abide is to remain, to dwell, to make a home. The Sacred Heart has made its home in us through these thirty-three days of devotion. Now we are called to make our home in the Sacred Heart. This mutual indwelling — we in Christ and Christ in us — is the ultimate fruit of devotion. It is the fulfillment of all the promises. It is the realization of all that Jesus desires for us: to be with him where he is, to dwell in his love forever.

As you complete these thirty-three days, think of this as a beginning. You have been formed by the Sacred Heart. You have encountered healing, strengthening, and sanctifying. Now you are invited to abide — to make your permanent dwelling in the love that has formed you. The promises of the Sacred Heart are fulfilled in those who remain faithful. Let your name be written in the Sacred Heart of Jesus, never to be blotted out.

Prayer

Sacred Heart of Jesus, dwelling place of divine love:
Establish peace in my home
and in every place where your image is honored.
Write my name in your heart, never to be blotted out.
Let me abide in you as you abide in me.
Make me a dwelling place for your love, now and forever.
As I complete these thirty-three days,
seal in me all that you have begun,
and keep me faithful to this devotion
all the days of my life.
Amen.

Today's Mantra

Sacred Heart of Jesus, I abide in you and you in me.

EPILOGUE

Sacré-Coeur

Thirty-three days. So what happens now?

You keep going. Not thirty-three days and you're done, but thirty-three days and now the devotion deepens. The pattern for this kind of fidelity was set in stone — literally — on a hill in Paris.

In 1870, France suffered defeat in the Franco-Prussian War. The following year brought the Paris Commune, which rose and fell in violence. Catholic leaders saw in these twin disasters divine judgment for decades of moral decline since the French Revolution's assault on the Church. Priests had been martyred, religious orders suppressed, and France's Catholic heritage torn apart.

In January 1871, a wealthy Catholic named Alexandre Legentil made a vow to build a church dedicated to the Sacred Heart as an act of national repentance. His brother-in-law Hubert Rohault de Fleury joined him. The National Assembly approved the project in 1873, declaring that France needed "to efface by this work of expiation the crimes which have crowned our sorrows."[27]

The site they chose was Montmartre, literally the "mount of martyrs." There, high above Paris where the entire city could see it, construction of the Basilica of the Sacré-Coeur began in 1875. It continued for nearly forty years. When the basilica was completed in 1914, it stood as a permanent offering, its white stone gleaming like a beacon of hope.

Since August 1, 1885 — even before the basilica was finished — perpetual adoration has continued without interruption. Day and night, someone is always before the Blessed Sacrament. One person finishes, another begins. For well over a century now, through two World Wars and waves of secularization, the adoration has never stopped.

That basilica is a national shrine for France. But more than that it is a claim: The Sacred Heart is the true heart of France. The nation built this monument to declare that its identity, its center, its deepest reality belongs to the Sacred Heart of Jesus.

You can make the same claim about your home. Not with a basilica but by enthroning an image of the Sacred Heart there and returning to it day after day in continual devotion. When you do this, you are declaring that the Sacred Heart is the true heart of this household. This is not magic or superstition. It is a visible sign of an invisible reality — a claim upon the space you inhabit that it belongs to him and has been given over to his reign.

But you may also claim this for your own interior life. What the basilica claimed for France, what the image claims for your household, you may claim for your heart. The true shrine is not made of stone but of flesh. It is the heart beating in your chest. Offered to the Sacred Heart and returned to daily in continual devotion, it becomes the dwelling place for divine love. Your heart becomes what you claim it to be: a place where the Sacred Heart reigns.

This is what these thirty-three days were preparing you for. Saint Margaret Mary saw the Sacred Heart aflame. Jesus told her that his heart could no longer contain its fire — it had to pour out into human hearts. He was looking for hearts willing to receive that flame, to let it burn, to become what they adore. He has been waiting for your heart.

The purpose of devotion to the Sacred Heart is not to make you feel pious. It is to conform you to him: gentle and humble of heart, burning with love that endures, able to hold both glory and sorrow without turning away. These thirty-three days were formation. What comes next is fidelity.

Each year, the Church celebrates the solemnity of the Sacred Heart on the Friday after Corpus Christi, and on that day it is fitting to renew your consecration to the Sacred Heart. But do not wait for June to live this devotion. Live it tomorrow when you wake, and the day after, and every day until your last breath. This is the pattern: continual return, continual offering, continual devotion to the Sacred Heart who continually pours out his love.

When you are ready — today, or on the solemnity, or at whatever moment the Spirit moves you — make this consecration your own. Saint Margaret Mary wrote out this consecration in a letter to another sister at the Moulins monastery. She knew what it cost to give everything to the Sacred Heart, and she also knew the great reward. Let her prayer become yours.

Act of Consecration to the Sacred Heart of Jesus[28]

I give and consecrate to the Sacred Heart of our Lord Jesus Christ my person and my life, my actions, pains, and sufferings, so that I may be unwilling to make use of any part of my being other than to honor, love, and glorify the Sacred Heart. This is my unchanging purpose, namely, to be all His, and to do all things for the love of Him, at the same time renouncing with all my heart whatever is displeasing to Him.

I therefore take You, O Sacred Heart, to be the only object of my love, the guardian of my life, my assurance of salvation, the remedy of my weakness and inconstancy, the atonement for all the faults of my life, and my sure refuge at the hour of death.

Be then, O Heart of goodness, my justification before God the Father, and turn away from me the strokes of His righteous anger. O Heart of love, I put all my confidence in You, for I fear everything from my own wickedness and frailty, but I hope for all things from Your goodness and bounty. Consume in me all that can displease or resist You. May Your pure love imprint You so deeply upon my heart, that I may never forget You or be separated from You.

I beseech You, through Your infinite goodness, grant that my name be engraved upon Your Heart, for in this I place all my happiness and all my glory, to live and to die as one of Your devoted servants.

Amen.

Notes

1. Margaret Mary Alacoque, *The Autobiography of Saint Margaret Mary*, trans. The Sisters of the Visitation (TAN, 1995), 163–164.

2. Ibid., 164.

3. Ibid.

4. Ibid.

5. Émile Bougaud, *The Life of St. Margaret Mary Alacoque* (TAN, 2002), 168–169.

6. Ibid., 169.

7. Ibid., 176.

8. John Croiset, *The Devotion to the Sacred Heart*, trans. Patrick O'Connell (TAN, 1998), 243.

9. Alacoque, *The Autobiography of Saint Margaret Mary*, 163–164.

10. Louis-Marie Montfort, "Treasures of the Sacred Heart (Hymn 40)," in *God Alone: The Collected Writings of St. Louis Marie de Montfort*, trans. Patrick Gaffney (Montfort, 1987), 268.

11. Karl Rahner, "'Behold This Heart!': Preliminaries to a Theology of Devotion to the Sacred Heart," in *Theological Investigations*, trans. Cornelius Ernst et al. (Mary Immaculate College, 2000), 3:344.

12. Bougaud, *The Life of St. Margaret Mary Alacoque*, 169.

13. Maria Faustina Kowalska, *Diary: Divine Mercy in My Soul*, 3rd ed., trans. George W. Kosicki and Teresa Tomaszewska (Marian Press, 2003), no. 1.

14. Ibid., no. 742.

15. Pius XI, *Miserentissimus Redemptor*, 2026, Vatican.va, par. 2.

16. St. Pio of Pietrelcina, "Letter to Padre Agostino (August 1918)," in *Letters: Volume I, Correspondence with His Spiritual Directors (1910-1922)*, trans. Elvira DiFabio (Our Lady of Grace Capuchin Friary, 1980).

17. Rev. Paolo Carta, "Padre Pio and the Sacred Heart," in *Voice*

of Padre Pio magazine, June 1997, https://www.ewtn.com/catholicism/library/padre-pio-and-the-sacred-heart-13848.

18. Bougaud, *The Life of St. Margaret Mary Alacoque*, 165.

19. Pius XI, *Miserentissimus Redemptor*, par. 6.

20. Augustine, *Expositions of the Psalms 73–98*, trans. Maria Boulding, III, *The Works of Saint Augustine: A Translation for the 21st Century* (New City, 2002), 86.5.

21. Irenaeus of Lyons, *Against Heresies*, ed. Alexander Roberts et al. (Ex Fontibus, 2012), IV.20.7.

22. Pius XI, *Miserentissimus Redemptor*, par. 6.

23. Augustine, *Expositions of the Psalms 73–98*, III, 86.5.

24. Bougaud, *The Life of St. Margaret Mary Alacoque*, 165.

25. Alacoque, *The Letters of St. Margaret Mary Alacoque*, specifically Letters 86 (promise 12), 132 (promises 6, 7, and 8), 35 (2 and 9), and 141 (1, 3, 4, 5, 10, and 11). A collected list of the promises is available here: "12 Promises of the Sacred Heart | EWTN," EWTN Global Catholic Television Network, https://www.ewtn.com/catholicism/library/12-promises-of-the-sacred-heart-13683.

26. Letter 33 in Alacoque, *The Letters of St. Margaret Mary Alacoque*.

27. David Harvey, *Paris, Capital of Modernity* (Routledge, 2003), 320.

28. See Alacoque, *The Autobiography of Saint Margaret Mary*, 117–118.